THE EVOLUTION OF GODS

Dr Ajay Kansal is a professor and consultant pathologist. It was during his medical practice that he encountered human suffering in a big way that made him question the concept of gods and drove him to write this book.

Advance Praise for *The Evolution of Gods*

'*The Evolution of Gods* is a more interesting book than most fiction I've looked at recently. Ajay Kansal has done a masterful job of putting forward his argument that God was invented by man. He shows the scientific reasons behind the creation of religion in a way that makes sense and follows the historical record. That a lot of research went into this book is evident and will be appreciated by readers. It was a fascinating read.'

– John Breeden, author, journalist and TV reporter

'This book is well-written and will surely stimulate discussion and debate. It will please some. It will anger and frustrate others. But one thing is certain, it will be bought, read and discussed with great frequency. Has great national and international potential. The question of God is the essence of humanity. This book makes a thoughtful attempt at setting forth a number of theories about the origin of God.'

– John Presta, author of *Mr. and Mrs. Grassroots: How Barack Obama, Two Bookstore Owners, and 300 Volunteers Did It*

'This is a fascinating and point-to-point compilation of ancient peoples' beliefs, discoveries, and possible explanations. It can be followed by a wide readership. The research seems well-done. The charm of this is the logical process used and the ability to imagine the primitive peoples.'

– Katherine L. Holmes, author of *The House in Windward Leaves*

'I am speechless. I don't have the words to say how much I enjoyed the book. The writing is straightforward, the author very knowledgeable about the subject, and he provides such wonderful examples from around the world. Finally there is a book that puts forth the logical and scientific evidence that religion and gods are manmade.'

– Susan Brauner, author of *The Adventures of Sohi*

'A very ambitious, concise and may be to some controversial subject. Well written and referenced work.'

— **Gretchen Steen, author of *Drágön Spawn***

'Here's to "lighting a candle in the darkest corner of human consciousness". I do think this is a fascinating book and well written!'

— **Michaela Foster Marsh, actor, singer and author of *The Matoke Tree***

'A very bold and fascinating book, well written and to the point. Very much enjoyed the way Dr Kansal presents historical situations and thesis. An excellent read that gives one reason to think. Well done!'

— **Mark Schietinger, author of *From the Edge, Rising***

'It is a very interesting and clearly explained subject. I enjoyed reading this.'

— **Wendy Jones, author of *Cinderella Girl***

'I read the book and it is a good start to demystifying humanity's struggle with mortality.'

— **Roberta E. Winter, author of *Unraveling US Healthcare***

'I wish I had seen this book when I was doing my study on mythology last semester. I have yet to read such fascinating questions and concepts.'

— **Amanda Paulger, author of *Kin of the Owl***

'I am fascinated by the concepts mentioned in the Preface, which is well-written, in a way a layman can understand. Such a self-contained, methodical treatise must have taken great care to compose.'

— **Jane Bwye, author of *Breath of Africa***

'In dark ages people were best guided by religion, as in a pitch-black night a blind man is the best guide; he knows the roads and paths better than a man who can see. When daylight comes, however, it is foolish to use blind old men as guides.'

– German poet Heinrich Heine

The Evolution of Gods

The Scientific Origin of Divinity and Religions

AJAY KANSAL

HarperCollins *Publishers* India

First published in India in 2012 by
HarperCollins *Publishers* India

Copyright © Ajay Kansal 2012

ISBN: 978-93-5029-438-3

4 6 8 10 9 7 5 3

Ajay Kansal asserts the moral right to be identified
as the author of this work.

The views and opinions expressed in this book are the author's own and the facts are
as reported by him, and the publishers are not in any way liable for the same.

All rights reserved. No part of this publication may be reproduced,
stored in a retrieval system, or transmitted, in any form or by any means,
electronic, mechanical, photocopying, recording or otherwise,
without the prior permission of the publishers.

HarperCollins *Publishers*
A-75, Sector 57, Noida, Uttar Pradesh 201301, India
77-85 Fulham Palace Road, London W6 8JB, United Kingdom
Hazelton Lanes, 55 Avenue Road, Suite 2900, Toronto, Ontario M5R 3L2
and 1995 Markham Road, Scarborough, Ontario M1B 5M8, Canada
25 Ryde Road, Pymble, Sydney, NSW 2073, Australia
31 View Road, Glenfield, Auckland 10, New Zealand
10 East 53rd Street, New York NY 10022, USA

Typeset in Adobe Garamond 10.5/13.5
InoSoft Systems Noida

Printed and bound at
Thomson Press (India) Ltd.

Contents

Preface ix
Chronology xiii
Life after Death 1
The Birth of Gods 18
Learning to Survive 32
Learning to Write 44
Sacrifice: Bribing the Gods 54
Gods and Demons of Diseases 67
Hinduism 103
Judaism 135
Christianity 144
Origin of Life 151
Why Gods Are Still Alive 163
Conclusion 199
Select Bibliography 209
Acknowledgements 215

Preface

Today we are all aware of the achievement of science. The population of the world is thriving as various scientific discoveries have provided food, water, health, security, comfort, recreation and much more to modern men. Mankind could achieve all this through a gradual learning process over hundreds of generations. Apart from needs and luxuries, scientists have solved many age-old mysteries too.

Since time immemorial, mankind has been anxious to know who created the first man and woman on the earth. Were they made by some supernatural power as most religious texts aver? Anthropologists have devoted decades to the study of the development of man dating back to the prehistoric age. And they have concluded without a trace of doubt that mankind was not created by some almighty power. On the contrary, it is man who created different gods.

This book is an attempt to scientifically explain why, when, how and where religions came into vogue. What kinds of suffering made people bow down before unseen powers – gods? When were gods created? Who invented morals and methods of worship? Who wrote the ancient scriptures? *The Evolution of Gods* is an attempt to put together anthropological and historical facts about the development of religions. The facts mentioned here have been cited from standard textbooks. These references are listed at the end of the book. All efforts have been made not to hurt anyone's personal feelings. If some text unwittingly hurts someone, I extend my sincere apologies in advance.

Around the time the human race came into being – between two and four hundred thousand years ago – people lived like wild animals. They were not aware of any god or demon. Around one hundred thousand years ago, the great invention of language changed the destiny of the human race. With the help of language, people began discussing events unfolding around them. Whatever they could not explain, the priest of their group attributed to some unseen power.

Mankind adopted religious practices to wrestle with events beyond its control, such as diseases, natural disasters and deaths. Priests worldwide began to advocate the worship of powers which were beyond human control, but could either harm or help them. Mankind came to believe that worshipping an unfathomable power could protect it and hence it sought the blessings of that power. Priests all over the world came up with almost identical methods of worship, such as folding hands, bowing, kneeling, offering of flowers, prayers, sacrifices, etc., in an attempt to flatter the powers and ask for their mercy. Later, priests designated these powers as gods. History demonstrates that whenever mankind faced a new challenge, priests discovered a more useful deity and consigned the older god to oblivion.

Around 3,000 years ago and later, mankind confronted new diseases such as cholera, tuberculosis, typhoid, plague, etc. Not only bodily diseases, population explosion also gave rise to social diseases such as poverty, inequality, injustice, crime and exploitation.

People lived in hell-like conditions. Prophets such as the Buddha, Moses, Jesus, etc., discovered the causes and remedies of human suffering. Many priests wrote about the teachings and stories of these prophets after their death. Ancient holy books such as the Bible and the Buddhacharita are compilations of such writings. These books advised worship, sacrifices, magic or morals to eradicate human miseries. These ancient holy books fashioned the organized religions of today.

Mankind suffered from diseases for three thousand years without doing enough to find out their causes and remedies. Have you ever wondered why? Priests discouraged writing and reading of scientific books. For a long period, priests convicted and punished several secular philosophers and scientists. They delayed scientific progress for two millennia. However, they could not impede it forever. Science ultimately had its way. Gradually, over the last two hundred years or so, scientists have managed to explain almost all these so-called divine powers. Today, science guides every aspect of human life. Surprisingly, mankind is still thanking someone in the sky for all these scientific developments!

The priestly class also misinterpreted the holy books to give rise to religious fundamentalism. No child is ever born displaying any trace of its religion anywhere on its body. But society tattoos the name of the religion on it. To eradicate fundamentalism, the new generations must learn when, why and how gods and religions were created. They must know the scientific aspect of the concept of gods. This knowledge might vaccinate new generations against the disease of fundamentalism.

During my medical practice, I have come across major human suffering which drilled a hole in my faith in gods. Besides, in a world marked by terrorism, poverty, inequality, exploitation, injustice, crimes, etc., how is it possible to envision a kind and loving God?

Gradually, I realized that a belief in gods and religious practices makes us superstitious and often leads people to inaction in the hope of a miracle.

The faith in supernatural powers takes away our willingness and ability to wrestle with sufferings such as poverty and illness; we usually blame our past karma. Our present sufferings have nothing to do with the karmas of our past lives, if indeed we have had past lives. And there is very little that gods can do, if anything at all, to relieve us of suffering.

As I read books that deal with human suffering and on the question of gods, I realized that gods and religions arose out of human imagination. I studied anthropology and the history of religions to find answers to the questions that plagued me. What I found out attested to my previous conception that it was man who created gods and not the other way round. I could not resist sharing what I have learned with others.

Have you ever thought why there are many religions but only one science on the earth? Truth is one but lies can be many. Mankind has to conceive a global religion of humanity. The human race created and worshipped gods as its creator and nurturer. Science has not yet identified any supernatural power that creates, governs, punishes or rewards human beings. This book is an effort to light a candle in the darkest corner of human consciousness.

Ajay Kansal
New Delhi,
November 2011

Chronology

Years Ago	Event
4.55 billion	A fiery ball-like portion separates from the sun
3.8–3.0 billion	The ball cools and unicellular creatures originate in oceans
3.0–2.0 billion	Origin of blue-green algae, bacteria and oxygen
500 million	Jawless fish, wingless insects, ozone layer
400–300 million	Insects, fish, frogs, reptiles, land plants
200–150 million	Birds, mammals, dinosaurs, flowers
100–10 million	Dinosaurs extinct, whales, monkeys, chimpanzees
2–1 million	Homo erectus, stone tools, use of fire
0.4–0.2 million	Modern human, invention of axe, hearth
0.1 million	Invention of language, practice of burials, sacrifices
100–50 thousand	Priests, elaborate burials, ornaments, herbal drugs

30 thousand	The last Ice Age, leather, footwear, huts with hearths
25 thousand	Idols of goddesses, cave art, ivory jewellery, ropes, knives
10 thousand	End of the Ice Age, explosion of human population
10–8 thousand	Agriculture, domestication, bow and arrow, canoe, pottery
8–5 thousand	Villages, towns, civilizations, sun temples, magic, alcohol
6–4 thousand	Writing, legal code, bricks, clothes, copper, wheel, phallus worship, libraries, goddesses
5–3.5 thousand	Hinduism, Rig Veda, iron, population explosion, cities
3.5–2.5 thousand	Judaism, Jewish Bible, epidemics like plague, cholera
2.5–2 thousand	The Buddha, democracy, monotheism, Hippocrates, Plato, Epicurus, philosophy, Ramayana, Mahabharata, money
2–1.5 thousand	Jesus Christ, Christian Bible, paper, clock, compass
1.5–1.0 thousand	Prophet Muhammad, Islam, Koran, crop rotation, gunpowder

1

Life after Death

The year 1698 CE was a milestone for the development of science; this year a British scientist and physician Edward Tyson dissected a chimpanzee and studied its internal organs. He was surprised to see its close resemblance to man. He asked himself why the organs of chimp and man were similar. Were men similar to chimps at some point in time? Did bygone generations of chimps give rise to mankind? Tyson was probably the first scientist to foresee that apes could be the ancestors of men.

In 1809 CE, Jean Bapiste Lamarck, a French naturalist, suggested the possible explanation of the evolution of animals. In 1859 CE, another naturalist, Charles Darwin proposed a well-crafted theory that plants and animals were not the same in the past. Before Darwin, it had been believed that God created all living beings in six days in the shapes and sizes that are seen today. Darwin was the first scientist who disproved this theory. He suggested that living beings originated as small and simple organisms. They gradually evolved into big plants and animals. Darwin explained how small fishes developed into larger ones, lizards into crocodiles, donkeys into horses, chimps into men and so on.

Lamarck also explained his theory through a few examples. For instance, millions of years ago, giraffes were as tall as horses. Their groups comprised giraffes of various heights. During adverse weather, it became difficult to find grass in the forest. Only the taller giraffes could reach to the leaves of higher trees. Therefore, they thrived and reproduced more successfully than the shorter giraffes. Thus, the number of tall giraffes increased with each new generation. Gradually, after thousands of generations, the height of giraffes increased. No scientist could observe this change in his/her lifetime because a noticeable increase in the height of giraffes took many millennia.

To visualize the evolution of animals, scientists took the help of palaeontology. Worldwide, scientists studied old fossils to explore the past. Many techniques such as carbon dating were invented to detect such as the age of fossils. These techniques could precisely detect how many years ago a body was alive on earth. Apart from establishing the age, modern scientists can now also interpret the lifestyle, diseases and the cause of death of any excavated dead body.

From the study of fossils, scientists can clearly visualize the evolution of animals. Modern palaeontology has proved Darwin's theory. Today, scientists have established that animals and plants were not created by God. They have explored precisely how life originated on the earth. Scientific theory of origin of life is discussed in the last chapter of the book.

Today, anthropologists have established that the human race evolved from Homo erectus that was a big ape-like creature. This evolution was a gradual process; scientists have definite evidence of almost each landmark of physical evolution such as both the body and the brain size. Regarding mental evolution, anthropologists have visualized the thoughts of the prehistoric people on the basis of their challenges and crafted implements. Furthermore, to understand the prehistoric mind, they have taken clues from the thought process of many aboriginals. Anthropologists believe that the human race came into being between 400,000 and 200,000 years ago. In that period, there were no man-made political boundaries. Instead, geographical barriers such as mountains or oceans limited human movement. Men lived as nomads or wanderers in groups or bands of fifty to hundred members.

During that time, people used fire and stone tools frequently. They had not yet discovered how to cultivate crops. They ate wild vegetables, fruits and animals. Therefore, men were always looking for the places rich in vegetation and animals. Whenever they faced scarcity of food, they searched for another rich forest. They had not yet learnt language, dressing, homemaking, morals and religion. Men led this life for a long period. Anthropologists believe that people of that period had developed imagination.

Imagination, a unique ability, made it possible for men to think beyond their visible, audible or other sensory experiences. It is difficult to ascertain when the human race evolved imagining. Their erect posture is also believed to have helped them in imagination. Man is probably the only animal species that has the ability to imagine. In fact, other animal species can see, hear, smell or feel their natural predators, which help them protect themselves. They have sensory organs to appreciate physical energies such as light or heat. But they cannot perceive a non-physical presence such as a ghost. To perceive a ghost, one has to be imaginative.

Man could perceive some unseen, unheard, untouchable, non-aromatic divine power only after the evolution of his imagination. Lack of imagination is the reason why no other animal has ever perceived divine powers such as demons and gods. Not only ghosts or gods, imagination also gave rise to all scientific inventions.

Around 100,000 years ago, the human race discovered language. This altogether changed human life. It differentiated men from animals. It was the first step towards the scientific advancements of today. With the help of this discovery, mankind radically changed the face of the earth. Men could perceive gods and demons only after they invented language.

Language was the medium for sharing or communicating information from one person to another. For ages, people shared their basic feelings such as fear, hunger or sexual desire only through crude sounds and gestures. All the members of a group understood these sounds and gestures. Thus the basic feelings of one person was communicated to others. However, without language men could not share most of their thoughts, emotions, etc.

When and why did men begin to talk through language? The Bible mentions that God Himself taught speech to Adam – the first man. Had it been true, there would have been only one language in the world. Although the Bible further explains that, at one point in time, God confounded human languages, this explanation seems to be an interpolation. In fact, language was an art that developed gradually. Many human groups invented their own languages independently to share their feelings, experiences, problems, etc. Many anthropologists believe that languages began developing around 100,000 years ago.

The earliest human language was similar to the utterances of a baby. Initially, people named many things around them – the nouns. Later, they named actions – the verbs. After this, they made sentences of two words by joining one noun and one verb. Gradually, their vocabulary increased. Around 30,000 years ago, men learnt to make sophisticated devices such as needles, cave paintings, jewellery, etc. Many such devices crafted in that period have been excavated and studied. Manufacture of these devices must have required discussion. Obviously, craftsmen of these devices had evolved a well-developed language.

Let's try to imagine the impact of language on the lifestyle of people. It must have radically changed their lifestyle, especially the upbringing of children. With language, men could share their feelings, experiences, problems and dreams with each other. Thus, each new human generation received the experience of their forefathers. That is what we call education today.

On the contrary, other animals can only guide their children to procure food. Without language, they cannot share their past experiences. Unlike humans, these animals survive through their own experiences because they cannot learn from their ancestors.

To understand this great change, just imagine a monkey who accidentally slips into a river. The monkey somehow manages to come out and soon, it develops a phobia of the river. It avoids going near that river for the rest of its life. The monkey expresses its fear to its family and friends by sounds and gestures. Since the monkey cannot narrate the whole episode, its children will never know the reason behind its river phobia. If a similar accident happens to a man, he can describe it to his family and friends with the help of language. Thus, men can teach their experiences to new generations.

After inventing language, men discussed everything that happened around them. They talked about seasons, rains, winds, clouds, plants, animals, etc. They observed that many events were beyond their understanding and knowledge. For example, they could not understand childbirths, deaths, seasons, storms, etc. These unpredictable events were always followed by helplessness, confusion and fear. Without language, each person pondered over such issues individually.

With the help of language, all members of the band discussed the reasons behind such events. For whatever they could not understand they blamed some unseen power. All the members gave their opinion. The opinion of the head of the band must have been given the maximum importance.

Later, this head came to be called priest. These priests imagined many unseen powers behind all natural events. For example, priests imagined that some power in the sky caused storms and rain. Besides, priests observed that there were two types of events, bad and good. Priests assumed that good and bad events were a result of bliss and anger of the powers respectively.

After this belief took firm shape, priests initiated a search for ways to appease those powers. Priests supposed that whatever pleases them would also please those powers. Therefore, priests invented many methods of flattering or worshiping them. For example, they preached folding of hands, bowing, kneeling, begging for mercy, etc. Gradually, each human group adopted a uniform way of worship to please these powers. These were performed under the guidance of priests. Besides, priests performed sacrifices to protect the people from the wrath of such powers. Anthropologists believe that these social activities were the beginning of religion.

These religious activities were performed by all the members of each human group and continued by their subsequent generations. The discovery of language facilitated this transmission of rituals and activities from one individual to another. From this premise, writer Nicholas Wade states:

> 'Like most behaviours that are found in societies throughout the world, religion must have been present in the ancestral human population before the dispersal from Africa 50,000 years ago. Although religious rituals usually involve dance and music, they are also very verbal, since the sacred truths have to be stated. If so, religion, at least in its modern form, cannot pre-date the emergence of language. It has been argued earlier that language attained its modern state shortly before the exodus from Africa. If religion had to await the evolution of modern, articulate language, then it too would have emerged shortly before 50,000 years ago.'

After learning language, men began to practise a primitive religion, but they had not yet learnt to write. So there is no written evidence of this religion. The religion practised before the advent of writing is known as prehistoric religion. Anthropologists were able to reveal this religion through the footprints of religious practises of that time. For example, they studied burials, human and animal sacrifices, clay figures and rock arts of the period. Although rare, these are well preserved and more authentic than any written account and helped anthropologists learn about this period of human development.

The earliest evidence of religious practices was excavated from the Skhul Cave situated at Mount Qafzeh in Israel. At this site, anthropologists found human skeletons, buried around 100,000 years ago. These dead bodies were buried along with stone tools, deer antlers and other animal bones. The graves also contained red ochre – a pigment commonly used for rituals.

The people of Skhul were the first to intentionally bury their dead. The vocal cords of the buried individuals were similar to those of modern humans. This attests that they had developed spoken language. Around 50,000 years ago and onwards, anthropologists have excavated more elaborate burials at many other places. They found many dead bodies painted with red ochre and buried with food, stone tools and animal bones. Gradually, people elaborated the burials. Graves of later periods contained many articles other than food and tools.

Anthropologists observed that all the dead bodies of each distinct human group were buried in an almost similar fashion. Although language was necessary for burials, it was not enough to facilitate consistent activity of a band after each death. All the buried people must not have died on one single day. There must have been a difference of months to years, or at least days, between two deaths.

For similar burials there must be one person to execute every burial. Without that person, different dead bodies could have been buried differently. That specific person must have been a head or priest of the band. Thus, by the time men began burying their dead, there was a priest in each band. The band of Skhul must have had such a priest to perform burial rituals.

All over the globe, enough evidence has been excavated to prove that there was a priest in each nomadic band. For example, decorative beads as old as 80,000 years were excavated from the Blombos Cave in South Africa. These beads were made of shells. Each bead shows a hole made by some stone tool. These beads were carved to make a necklace. Anthropologists believe that some priest might have worn such a necklace.

The dead body of a sixty-year-old man has been excavated from Sungir in Russia. He was buried around 30,000 years ago with unusual jewellery. His body was found with a big necklace made of five thousand beads. Both his arms were decorated with twenty-five bracelets of mammoth bone. Anthropologists have estimated that an artist of that period must have spent years to make his jewellery. They have concluded that this person must have been someone important, most likely the priest of the place.

A few excavated bodies indicate that these priests also took care of sick members of the band. For example, at Shanidar in modern Iraq, four bodies have been excavated which were buried around 60,000 years ago. One body (Shanidar 1) was a male who died at the age of forty-five. Surprisingly, his bones exhibited multiple fractures with signs of healing. He had lost an eye and a forearm. Probably he was injured by some falling rock.

Shanidar 1 was a rare corpse that displayed both trauma and healing. The evidence of healing indicated that he must have been injured well before his death. Now the question arises, who helped him in the healing process? The people of Shanidar must have had a priest who bandaged and immobilized the fractured bones of his men.

The above facts indicate that the people of Shanidar looked after their sick and aged. Besides, the priests treated the patients with herbal medicines as well. Another dead body (Shanidar 2) was a male who died at the age of forty. He was buried with routine rituals and seven flowers of specific medicinal properties. Today, these flowers are known to have diuretic, stimulant, astringent, anti-inflammatory and other curative properties. Obviously, the priest of Shanidar had knowledge of herbal drugs. Thus, all the above facts together attest that each nomadic band had a priest who buried the dead and also treated the sick.

In the last one hundred years, scientists have studied many isolated tribal people – aboriginals. These tribals led a primitive life. Each such tribe also had a priest similar to the priests of prehistoric nomadic people. Priests of the nomadic people can be better visualized with the knowledge of tribal priests and excavated evidence mentioned above. Thus, the priest of prehistoric people can be portrayed as follows.

The priest was the most intelligent man of each nomadic band. He was the scientist of each group. In fact, the priest was the leader of the group. He acquired knowledge from his parents and from his own experiences. He knew how to ignite and utilize fire. Generations of priests must have been instrumental in the invention and teaching of languages.

The priest invented better tools to kill animals and protect his group. He also planned the hunting of animals. He decided the role of each member during a big hunt. Whenever his group faced scarcity of food he guided them to a new forest. He knew the whereabouts of wild animals.

He treated the injured and the sick. Generations of priests invented and accumulated the knowledge of herbal medicines. This was not an easy job during prehistoric times. He had no books or other sources of knowledge. He had to find out herbs and experience their good or bad effects himself. He invented rituals to bury the dead and pacify their souls.

The priest considered himself to be different from others of the group. To express this, he adorned his body differently. He covered his head with a cap made of feathers, beads, etc. He decorated his neck with garlands. Besides, he painted his forehead with coloured pastes. Human skulls, bones and feathers were his favourite possessions.

The priest was the embodiment of the saying 'Nothing succeeds like success'. The priest got more and more opportunities to prove his ability. His success was the result of his wisdom, but people believed that he had divine powers. They consulted him regularly before any new venture. He invented many tricks to keep their faith intact which were perceived by the common people as magical.

Magic tricks performed by prehistoric priests can be better illustrated by an example. Naskapi was a tribal group living in the Labrador region of Canada. People consulted their priest before each venture. For example, before hunting, they asked the priest where they could get animals easily. For this, the priest held a flat bone over the sacred fire as if the bone was a map. After this, the priest chanted, 'May lord guide us about the direction of hunt.' After a few minutes, irregular cracks appeared in the bone. The priest forecasted that people would find animals in the direction of the crack. Next day, hunters searched animals in that direction. Usually, they found and killed some animal. If they failed, the priest explained that they must have made some mistake.

Similarly, many priests invented magical ways of forecasting the direction of a hunt. With time, the supremacy of the priest over other members was unanimously established. He was considered the interpreter of natural events and dreams. After each mysterious event, his explanation and remedy was widely accepted. It was the priest who invented and nourished the concepts of life after death, the soul, ghost, gods and other inexplicable matters.

With this knowledge about prehistoric priests, it is now possible to imagine a scene after a death about 100,000 years ago. By then, people had begun nursing patients. Whenever a patient stopped moving, they called their priest to heal the sick. The priest tried all remedies known to him for hours to revive the patient. People were puzzled to see that their beloved friend was not breathing, moving or talking. The priest continued to care for him for a few more days in the hope that he might return to life. The band members gathered around the patient and talked about the good times they spent with that person. In the meantime, they smelt a foul smell from the body. People were already sad, and now they could not even sit there. They lost any hope of his revival. They discussed this with the priest, who suggested shifting the body away from the caves.

Now, they had another concern – to protect the dead body from scavengers such as vultures. The priest advised covering it with soil. With the passage of time, priests began burying the dead bodies in a pit and covering it with soil. Burial was a foolproof method for keeping away both the scavengers and the bad smell. Gradually, almost all prehistoric human groups evolved one or the other method for burial or cremation. Priests taught these burial methods to subsequent generations.

Anthropologists have found two basic purposes behind burial of the dead: avoiding foul smell and safety of the dead body. Why did people desire to keep the dead body intact? Why did people provide sustenance for the dead body? Scientists believe that these people had developed a peculiar conviction about death. They believed in an afterlife. In other words, some sort of life survived even after death. Since some life remained after death, it became logical to keep the dead body intact and provide food. What was the reason behind this conviction? What happened after each death that was perceived as a glimpse of the remaining life?

In fact, with the help of language, priests and other wise men of each human group must have discussed the difference between a live and a dead body. The more they learnt about death, the more they were confused. They had many questions after each death: What was lacking in the body now? What was inside the body? Who was running it?

Whenever they killed some animal, they routinely noticed how it reacted after being hit. For example, after hunting a deer, people might have noticed and said, 'First hit, deer fell, still moving, head hit, movement stopped, life out.' They concluded that the blow on the head opened a way out for the life of the deer. After observing thousands of dying animals, priests concluded that there was something that kept the body of each animal alive and running.

At some point in time, priests imagined an unseen divine spark that governed animal bodies. Priests of every place named it; one of those names was soul. Each animal could live as long as its soul was in the body. After the soul departed from the body, the living thing died. Since the soul was invisible, no one could see it while it left the body.

This belief was not an individual perception but a global phenomenon. It is evident from the fact that all ancient and independently developed religions documented the same conviction. Even today, almost all the people under the sun believe that an invisible soul is running their body. Eminent anthropologist Edward Taylor has said: 'The belief in souls was the earliest form of religion.' He termed this belief as animism.

After the discovery of the soul, priests became curious about what happens to the soul after death. This question was answered by dreams. What are dreams? Whatever concerns you during the day is usually seen in dreams. Dreams are a reflection of the dreamer's thoughts and imagination. After each death, the close relatives of the dead missed them. Therefore, they dreamt about their beloved relative.

Imagine what kind of dreams an early man could have after the death of his mother? Hunger was the prime concern in those days. He might have dreamt of his mother asking for food. The son consulted the local priest about his dream. The priest explained that the hungry soul of his mother was wandering around. After this, whenever another person of the band died, the priest advised to keep food in his grave. Take yet another example. A son saw his frightened mother in his dreams and consulted the local priest. The priest interpreted that his mother's soul was scared of wild animals. Soon, the priest took a decision to include stone tools in future graves.

Dreaming about the dead gave rise to a conviction that the dead were still wandering around. Even after death, some unseen portion of the body survived – the soul. People envisaged that the soul would require utilities to sustain and protect itself. The burial articles were provided to fulfil the needs of the soul, the surviving life. Keeping food and stone tools in the graves was a lesson that men must have learnt over the millennia. Later, it became customary to provide all that one needed during one's lifetime in the grave.

According to Taylor, prehistoric people built many imaginary stories and myths about dreams and death. Gradually, these stories gave rise to religions. Taylor suggested that dreaming about the dead initiated the idea of the dual existence of all people: a visible physical body and an invisible soul. The idea of life after death and the soul was merely a product of human imagination. Over millennia it was transformed into a concept. This knowledge was communicated to each subsequent generation. Here again it is important to note, this complex information could be conveyed to children through language only.

The concept of the soul gave birth to the idea of ghosts. Later, ghosts became a global illusion. Almost all civilizations on the earth have endowed ghosts with almost similar attributes. Commonly, ghosts were believed to be wandering souls of the dead. Each ghost was supposed to be an unseen power that had the ability to disturb, destabilize or destroy people. At the same time, men could not physically hurt any ghost. Their body contained no physical or chemical substance. Therefore, it was not possible to see, touch, hear or smell them.

In fact, many bizarre human experiences gave birth to the idea of ghosts. Whenever men observed an unexplained event, the unseen power of some ghost was imagined to explain it. For example, it was believed that all sounds and lights with no obvious source, were produced by ghosts. Huge trees with aerial roots produced terrorizing sounds and sparks during strong winds. People considered these to be caused by ghosts. Even today, many big trees are believed to be resting places of ghosts.

Other than trees, ghosts were supposed to be wandering around graves. Due to this reason, people around the world were scared of graveyards. Several modern religions had similar concepts about souls and ghosts, while they had contradictory viewpoints about gods. Primitive men in dense forests already lived in fear of wild animals. Now, after dusk, another fear, that of ghosts, followed them.

The existence of burial rituals and priests as discussed earlier were the major evidence of prehistoric religion. Besides, anthropologists have glimpsed another aspect of prehistoric times in the Krapina Cave in Croatia. Here, they excavated seventy dead bodies buried around a 100,000 years ago. The skeletons showed deliberate marks of injuries inflicted by stone tools. A few skulls exhibited evidence of deliberate crushing.

Archaeologists have discovered a pit of bones of the same period at Atapuerca in Spain. The pit was found to be full of human and animal skeletons of different periods. Here also human bones showed similar marks of injuries inflicted by stone tools. These dead bodies are concrete evidence of cannibalism practised in those days.

Why did the people living around Atapuerca and Krapina Caves kill and eat their own kind? Dire scarcity of food seems a possible reason. However, there was no evidence to suggest that they were starving. The pit at Atapuerca contained skeletons of other animals too. Men could have eaten those animals rather than their own race. Anthropologists have many reasons to believe that these people practised ritual cannibalism. Rituals must have been dedicated to some of their gods. People must have killed their near and dear ones to please their gods.

Apart from these, archaeologists have also found evidence of idol worship in the prehistoric era. Many feminine idols have been excavated. These were carved around 20,000–30,000 years ago. Most of the sculptures depict a female figure with large breasts and protruding belly, indicating a pregnant female. The artists did not carve the facial features of these idols. This indicates that artists wished only to depict pregnancy.

Some anthropologists consider that these are idols of fertility goddesses. Others argue that these were the earliest male erotica. It is surprising that the statues excavated from the unconnected places exhibit more or less similar pregnant females. It is most likely that these idols did in fact depict fertility goddesses. A few idols were painted with red ochre, which also supports that these were idols of goddesses.

What could be the probable reason behind the worship of the sculptures of pregnant females? Randall White, professor of anthropology at New York University, has said: 'These figures date from a time (and such time must surely have existed) when early men had yet to make a link between sexual intercourse and childbirth.' At that time, birth would have been considered miraculous.

In fact, priests were scientists too. They observed everything around them, such as plants, animals, the sun, the sky, etc. They were unaware of the role of the sexual act in causing pregnancy. They observed that women alone had the capability of giving birth. Natural changes in pregnant women surprised them. They perceived pregnancy as a mysterious event. Childbirth, breastfeeding and even the menstruation cycle were amazing to them. Monthly bleeding without any obvious injury was frightening. In fact, women were mysterious and miraculous creatures for prehistoric men. Males found themselves incapable of giving birth to a new life. Through these idols, people must have worshipped the exceptional power of the female – power to create a new life.

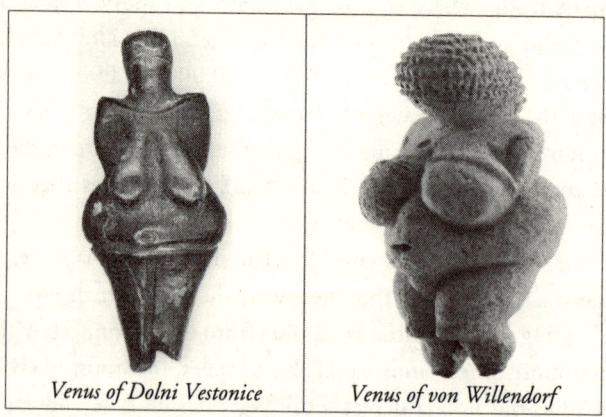

Venus of Dolni Vestonice   *Venus of von Willendorf*

Prehistoric Goddesses

Cave arts provide another evidence of prehistoric religion. Most of these carvings depict animals of hunt. Anthropologists believe that priests must have made these sculptures in anticipation of success in hunting.

Eminent anthropologist Peter Watson has written that there are three basic requirements of a religion. First, there must be a belief in life after death. Second, a few individuals, like priests, must claim to communicate with superhuman powers called gods. Finally, people must have the conviction that certain prayers and rituals can please the gods, who will then fulfil their wishes. During the prehistoric period, mankind had evolved all the three. It was the period when the human race formulated the concept of superhuman powers which they called gods. The gods the prehistoric people worshipped are discussed in the next chapter.

2

The Birth of Gods

The previous chapter talked about priests and burial rituals of prehistoric people leading a nomadic life. They buried their dead with food, stone tools, red ochre, flowers, etc. People kept food and tools for the dead to protect them from hunger and danger. However, the presence of red ochre and flowers in the graves still remained unexplained. These articles were useless for the dead. It is likely that they were dedicated to the gods they worshipped.

Who were the gods of the prehistoric people? What was the motive behind the ritual cannibalism practised by them? Whom did they wish to please by killing their beloved ones? Interestingly, palaeontologists have found many graves of prehistoric people, but there was rarely any evidence of idols or temples. They must have worshipped their gods without making idols.

In fact, the people, who initiated the practice of burying their dead, had already learnt to speak a primitive language. Men could learn to speak a discernible language only around 30,000 years ago. However, they had not yet learnt to write. Their religious activities can only be visualized from excavated dead bodies and the devices made by them.

Today, anthropologists can determine lifestyles, needs and challenges of prehistoric people from their excavated bodies. However, they cannot accurately interpret the thoughts of the dead. Therefore, the religious beliefs of the prehistoric people are not known precisely. There is only indirect evidence about their gods. Their gods can also be visualized through the knowledge of their challenges.

The prime challenge faced by these people was adverse weather. Favourable weather provided them food, water and comfort. During bad weather, they faced scarcity of the same. Many a time, adverse weather posed a life-threatening challenge.

Archaeologists have discovered that the earth has suffered many Ice Ages in the past. During the Ice Ages, the temperature of the earth was much lower than it is today. A major part of the surface of the earth was covered by snow. The snow locked a substantial amount of seawater on the ground. Therefore, the sea level decreased to one hundred metres below the present level.

The last Ice Age began around 30,000 years ago. Gradually, snow covered a major part of the surface of the Earth. Around 10,000 years ago, the Ice Age came to an end. Thus, the last Ice Age continued for 20,000 years. During that period, nights, being colder, were tough times. People spent their nights in temporary huts made of bamboos, wild grasses, bones or skins. Alternatively, they lived in rock-sheltered natural caves. They just had animal skins, barks of trees or large leaves to cover themselves. Thus, winter nights were life-threatening for the men living in the Ice Age.

Archaeologists have found many bone needles dating back to almost 30,000 years ago. These were stitching needles with an eye at one end. This indicates that craftsmen of these needles must have learnt to stitch. They had only animal skins to stitch; obviously, they wore leathers. These needles are the earliest evidence of men's clothing. In fact, men began to cover their bodies due to cold, not to hide or reveal the contours of their bodies!

Eminent physical anthropologist Erik Trinkaus has found evidence to indicate that the use of shoes began in the period between about 40,000 and 26,000 years ago. He observed that toe-bones of human fossils of this period were shorter and thinner. He concluded that wearing shoes resulted in less bone growth and ultimately in shorter and thinner toes.

People living in the last Ice Age were dependent upon forests for food. Snow ruined major forests of the earth. Many animals could not survive the cold. Thus, men could not procure enough food. To search for food, they had to change their habitations frequently. Therefore, men could not build permanent huts.

Many excavated dead bodies of the period exhibit evidence of injuries inflicted by wild animals. This indicates the danger posed by wild animals to them. Today, it is difficult to understand the misery they faced. Hunger, fear of wild animals, and winter nights were the prime challenges for the people living in the Ice Age.

Prehistoric people already knew fire; they had seen many accidental fires in the forest. They observed that this power could destroy even big trees. They considered the charred trees as victims of the anger of the power. They perceived fire as a power that could provide them with warmth like the sun; at the same time, it was mighty enough to char anything that came across its way. They noticed that all the wild animals were also scared of fire.

Men had discovered how to ignite fire by striking two stones well before they learnt spoken language. After language came into being, they must have discussed the different ways in which fire could help them. They must have discussed the uses and properties of fire at great length. During nights, fire was the only possible source of warmth, light and protection from wild animals. Igniting fire by striking two stones was a difficult and time-consuming task.

Therefore, once ignited, fire must have been considered a blessing of some divine power.

Men living in the last Ice Age invented the technique to maintain a running fire round the clock. Many nomadic bands of the period had one central hearth (fireplace). It was used to ignite a new fire every time. After sunset, people sat around the fireplace. Once they were asleep, its smoke warned wild animals about fire and thus protected the people throughout the night.

Hearths have been consistently excavated in the settlements of nomadic bands. For example, archaeologists have excavated an entire settlement of a nomadic band in the Czech Republic belonging to 25,000 years ago. The night shelter had four round huts made of animal skins and bones. The huts were built around a big open hearth, and each hut had its own hearth inside.

The discovery of fire and hearths empowered men against other animals. Even the most deadly carnivores such as tigers did not dare to come near human settlements. The utility of and difficulty in igniting fire elevated hearths to a divine status. Men of the last Ice Age must have worshipped hearths. This is further supported by the fact that there is enough historic evidence of fire worship.

For example, Hindus have been worshipping fire as a god for more than five thousand years. Yajna, a kind of fire worship, is still the core ritual for all occasions of the present-day Hindus. This worship is done through chanting of flattering poems addressed to the fire god. This fire worship must have started in the last Ice Age. Today, devotees of almost every religion ignite a fire before their prayers. This custom must have its roots in fire worship.

Now, let's imagine the daily schedule of prehistoric people during the Ice Age. A typical day began before sunrise. The crowing of a rooster was the only alarm clock to wake them up. Men came out of the small caves or huts wrapped in deerskin. Mornings were invariably colder, so they started shivering. Soon, they turned in the direction of the sunrise. They eagerly waited for sunlight to appear on the horizon. As soon as people saw the saffron light of dawn, they stood still for a sunbath. Their heads and hands faced the rising sun as if they were worshipping it. During many millennia of the last Ice Age, men spent their mornings in this posture.

After the sun revived their body, they ventured out to the forest nearby. They wandered all through the forest for food. The females usually collected fruits, nuts or roots from the forest. The males preferred hunting. Herbivores such as goat, lamb and cattle were their easy prey. Usually they did not chase animals, but patiently waited until the prey came within their reach. They held the lazy animal and hit it with a pointed stone tool. For faster animals, they threw pointed tools to injure the animal. If a stone hit the target, the job for the day was done. If the animal was lucky and escaped, they had to wait for another animal. Both luck and intellect were mandatory to kill animals. In order to survive, men had to outperform animals. In the afternoons, both men and women returned to their camp with the booty.

What did early men do after sunset? Unlike today, they did not have various means of recreation. They discussed everything in their world from the sun, the rivers, weather, plants, animals and everything around them. They were perplexed by the daily phenomenon of sunrise and sunset. They had many questions like: 'Why does everything become dark at night? Where does the sun go at night?' In the daytime, light helped them to find food and source of water. With the help of daylight, they could easily see wild animals. Faint visibility at night rendered them vulnerable to wild animals. At night they were in constant fear of wild animals.

People recognized that during daytime, sunlight empowered them. Thus, nights were the anxious periods for prehistoric people. It is well evident by one hymn of the Rig Veda. It narrates the people's fear during nights around five thousand years ago. It reads:

'Oh night, guard us from the wolf, guard us from the thief and so be good for us to pass.'

Thus, men concluded that day was a time of delight. They had neither the comfort of a cosy home nor the protection of clothes. During the Ice Age, the bright sunny days were happy days for men. They had to spend the cloudy days in their caves around the hearth. During the cloudy days, they discussed: 'Where has the sun gone today? Is the yellow ball relaxing in its cave? Why doesn't the sun shine every day?' These questions confused and haunted them.

Men appreciated that they were dependent on sunlight for warmth, gathering, hunting and protecting. People had no other equally potent source of light and warmth. After much discussions and observations, men concluded that their life was impossible without sunlight. Thus, during the last Ice Age, men must have identified the sun as their saviour.

At some point in time, we do not know exactly when this happened, mankind developed an instinct. Whenever men identified some power beyond their control that could harm or help them, they began to worship that power. They believed that worship protected them and sought the blessings of that power. All over the globe, people adopted similar methods of worship. For example, people worshipped by folding their hands, bowing, kneeling, offering flowers, praying, sacrificing, etc. During prayers, they sung flattering songs to seek the mercy of that power.

For the people of the last Ice Age, the sun was their saviour, and it was beyond their control. After attaining this knowledge, people must have initiated praying to the sun to seek its mercy. The earliest prayers of men must have involved flattering and thanking the sun in words. Initially, people spoke sentences of two to three words only. Their prayers would have been something like: 'Night bad, day good, thank sun, come daily.'

After the development of well-defined languages, people learnt to make more extensive sentences. By then, these slogans of two words must have been replaced by more exact expressions. For example, 'Almighty sun, kindly help us.' Gradually, these sentences were replaced by poems, rhymes or hymns.

Enough evidence indicates that ancient people chanted flattering poems for the sun at many places of the world. For example, around five thousand years ago, Indian priests composed the Gayatri Mantra to worship the rising sun. Since then, Hindus have been chanting this mantra. It is one of the many mantras composed by the priests to appease the sun. It reads: 'We meditate on the adorable glory of the radiant sun; may he inspire our intelligence.'

Similarly, around the same time, Mesopotamian priests composed the poem 'Enuma Elish' to worship the sun. Besides, priests of many other places also wrote poems to worship the sun. These are discussed at length in Chapter 4. Historians believe that these poems were composed and chanted millennia before they were written. This indicates that sun worship began in the last Ice Age.

There is palaeontological evidence as well about the solar worship practised by prehistoric people. For example, the remains of a nomadic band were excavated at Abu Hureyra on the Euphrates River in Syria. The band buried their dead in a similar fashion. All the bodies in their graves were facing east. Furthermore, the bodies were positioned similar to a child in its mother's womb. Anthropologists believe that the people must have had some motive behind this specific method of burial. Facing east, which is the direction of sunrise, indicates some prayer to the sun. Foetal position indicates that people were making appeal for a new birth for the dead. Thus, the people were praying to the sun for rebirth of the dead.

Another evidence of prehistoric solar worship is Stonehenge

at Salisbury in England. This exceptional monument was erected around five thousand years ago by prehistoric people. Archaeologists believe that the place was in use millennia before its erection. The monument had many erect stones. Scholars have studied and found that the stones were arranged in a specific pattern. These were used to observe solar changes. People predicted winter and summer solstices by observing the shadows cast by these stones.

Many scholars have concluded that it was a temple of the sun, and people assembled there for solar worship, sacrifices and ceremonies. Stonehenge is the oldest temple of the sun on earth. However, it does not display any stone idol of the sun. Not only Stonehenge, but many similar prehistoric solar observatories have also been excavated from the world. These monuments also do not have any solar icon. It is obvious that prehistoric people worshipped the actual sun without making its idols.

Let us also imagine the reaction of prehistoric men while they faced wind, cloud, thunder, lightning and rain. Imagine the previously discussed priest of the nomadic group living at Sungir in Russia, thirty thousand years ago. He used to wear heavy jewellery. Like all other priests, he must have been a keen observer. During his free time, he usually lay under a banyan tree and observed the moving leaves. One day he noticed a vigorous shaking of big trees. The priest concluded that some unseen power was moving the leaves, and he named it wind.

Not only wind, changes in the sky also amazed people of those days. While watching the sky on a clear day, the inquisitive priest observed the clouds floating in the sky. He noticed the size, shape and colour of the clouds. He further observed that these were not only moving but changing shape too. He predicted that this was yet another power of the sky. The priest noticed that usually the clouds and wind moved in the same direction. Thus he concluded that both the wind and the clouds were related.

One afternoon, the priest suddenly faced a strong wind. Even large trees began shaking. The aerial roots and dry branches of the old banyan tree were whistling. The priest smelt a pleasant aroma produced by drops of water on dry soil. Soon, the priest heard a loud clap of thunder that frightened him. The priest and others assembled and stared in the direction of the sound. They were surprised to see a flash of lightning with each clap of thunder.

Men of the time knew only two sources of light: the sun and fire. They were scared of accidental forest fires. This lightning in the sky terrified the whole band. The priest had already heard a few stories about storms and sky power from his forefathers. He had experienced many storms in his lifetime, but this was the most horrible one.

The intensity of the wind, thunder and lightning was increasing. Suddenly, they saw a very big and bright bolt of lightning. That almost reached the ground far from their dwelling. All of them stood frightened thinking about how to escape. Soon, it began raining heavily, which continued until late in the night.

Next morning, the sky was clear, but the fallen leaves carpeted every inch of the land. Many branches and small trees were seen on the ground. All these were the result of the disaster of the night. The priest was curious to see the place where the lightning bolt had struck the ground. He quickly moved in that direction. After a few kilometres he found a charred tree. He immediately summoned the whole band.

After this, the priest and others began discussing the possible reasons behind this destruction. How could the lightning have charred the tree? Soon, the priest visualized that the lightning bolt reached the ground and burnt the tree. To explain further, the priest must have imagined some power in the sky that appeared as thunder, lightning and rain. All this was enough to fabricate a story or myth about the sky power or god. Subsequent generations of the band were shown that charred tree as a victim of the wrath of the sky god. This way the myths about the visit of the sky god upon the earth continued for generations.

The nomadic bands, such as discussed above, usually wandered along riverbanks to procure regular water and food. However, proximity to the river exposed them to the constant danger of floods. Storms were commonly accompanied by heavy rain, which caused floods in nearby rivers. Floods destroyed huts and other man-made structures near riverbanks. During the Ice Age, snowfalls or hailstorms were common. This further lowered the temperature.

Rain often extinguished the fire of the hearths that were used to ignite fire. People could not even ignite a new fire with stones because rainwater drenched everything. Thus, it became increasingly difficult to ignite fire during rains. Besides, the clouds hid the sun. Thus, storm and rain was followed by a spell of cold wave. Many a storm in winter posed a big threat to the survival of the band. Thus, storms made human life miserable in the Ice Age.

After development of language, old men and priests of the bands discussed the disasters caused by storms. They looked upon a storm as a malevolent force. Therefore, they assumed that storms were an expression of the anger of the power residing in the sky, the sky god. They further noticed that during storms, lightning was always followed by thunder. They concluded that first the sky power appeared before them in the shape of lightning and then commanded them in the voice of thunder. They assumed that lightning followed by thunder was the synchronized manifestation of the sky god.

Thus, people and the priest together must have concluded that the anger of the sky god could endanger their lives. At the same time, the sky god was beyond their control. The priest was aware that worship was the only remedy to subside the anger of such a power.

With this knowledge, whenever the band heard a clap of thunder, everyone came out of their huts. The terrified band stared at the lightning in the sky. While people stood helpless, their wise priest would have called out to the sky god for help. He must have shouted slogans like 'forgive us, have mercy, stop it'. The people repeated these slogans until the storm passed. After the storm ceased, they must have believed that the sky god had heard their prayers.

Thus, people tried to seek the mercy of the sky god through their body language and slogans. Not only at one place, priests all over the world, composed similar stories about the sky god. The simple slogans were gradually replaced with long sentences and ultimately hymns or small poems.

For example, around five thousand years ago, Vedic priests composed many flattering hymns to escape the anger of the sky god. Hindus chanted the hymns of the sky god under the guidance of priests. Almost all the poems contain flattering statements addressed to the sky god. For example:

> Sky god Rudra, slay us not, nor abandon us.
> When thou art angry, let not thy noose seize us.
> Oh Rudra, you nourish all, heal all.
> We are chanting hymns in your glory,
> to protect us from your wrath.

Regarding the sky god, eminent author Karen Armstrong wrote, 'Some of the very earliest myths probably dating back to Palaeolithic period, were associated with the sky, which seems to have given people their first notion of the divine. Contemplating the sky filled people with dread and delight, with awe and fear. At some point—we do not know exactly when this happened—people in various far-flung parts of the world began to personify the sky.'

For example, the Jewish Bible, the Old Testament, has portrayed God in the attribute of the sky god. The bible mentions the story of mainly three prophets: Noah, Abraham and Moses. The first prophet Noah worshipped the god of rain – the sky god. The second prophet of the Bible was Abraham. Ancient literature mentions that Abraham also worshipped the sky god and other Canaanite deities.

According to *The Oxford Companion to World Mythology* (David Leeming, Oxford University Press, 2005, page 118), 'It seems almost certain that the God of the Jews evolved gradually from the Canaanite El, who was in all likelihood, the God of Abraham.'

The third prophet of the Bible was Moses. The Bible documents frequent meetings between Moses and his God Yahweh. The Bible has portrayed the attribute of God Yahweh similar to the sky god. For example, the fourth chapter the book Deuteronomy reads: 'Moses heard the voice of God, "Collect the people to hear my words, that they may learn to fear me all the days that they shall live upon the Earth, and that they may teach their children." People came and stood under the mountain burnt with fire into the midst of heaven, with darkness, clouds, and thick darkness. God spoke out form the midst of the fire. Moses heard the voice, but saw no similitude.

This depiction indicates that Moses encountered nothing extraordinary but a severe storm. Chapter 29 of Psalm also depicts Yahweh as a storm god. In fact, Moses must have coined the name 'Yahweh' for the power behind the expressions of the sky, such as wind, cloud, rain, lightning and thunder.

Scholar Mark S Smith has written that God Yahweh was the metamorphosis of the Canaanite sky god Baal (Hadad). Thus, all the prophets of the Jewish Bible were the worshipper of the sky god.

As late as in the eighteenth century, Benjamin Franklin discovered electricity in lightning. Today, everyone knows the cause of lightning. They can laugh at the fact that early men considered storms as the anger of the sky god. History mentions that this sky god frightened the people all over the globe. This god ruled the world for many millennia. This god was the most worshipped god of all ages.

Now, it is obvious that ancient people worshipped the sun, the sky and fire. This worship was done by flattering hymns addressed to these powers. Priests composed these sacred verses and taught them to every new generation. Everyone chanted these poems to worship the gods. Gradually, priests invented the art of writing and wrote these poems.

The oldest writings of the world comprised flattering poems dedicated to the sun, the sky and fire. While praying, these were chanted regularly under the guidance of priests. These writings are concrete evidence of worship of these gods. These writings are narrated at length in Chapter 4.

Historians believe that ancient writings were composed and chanted many millennia before being written. Prior to the invention of writing, these were passed onto subsequent generations through the oral tradition. Karen Armstrong has written that many myths about gods documented in ancient scriptures were initiated by prehistoric people. This proves that the prehistoric ancestors of the people who composed our ancient literature also had the same beliefs. Study of the above attests that all the ancient people conceived of similar gods and prayers. Obviously, people all over the world practised one religion. Today, it looks surprising that many unconnected human groups independently invented similar concepts. In fact, these concepts were adopted to wrestle with similar needs and challenges that mankind faced.

People learnt about religion in the same way they learnt to make tools, to ignite fire, to speak language and to do many more things. These prayers were not planned, imitated or revealed by any of the prophets. These developed spontaneously in thousands of human groups all over the world. In fact, men worshipped anything that could help or harm them. The next chapter describes the challenges faced by the human race at the end of the last Ice Age.

3

Learning to Survive

The previous chapters described how mankind invented many utilities after learning the art of communication. Men developed several useful tools such as the bow and arrow, small boats, hearths, etc. Besides, they invented leather, shelters, medicines, etc. These were the scientific discoveries of the time. People recognized the powers of the sun, the sky and fire and began to worship them as gods, thus giving rise to the early religions.

Better tools made hunting easier and equipped men to protect themselves from wild animals. With language, people could coordinate their bands to kill big animals as well. Leather, hearths, and better shelters protected them from the cold. Moreover, hearths protected them from wild animals. Herbal drugs and better care of the sick further increased their lifespan.

All these factors together led to a population explosion. Anthropologists have estimated that 100,000 years ago, human population on the earth was around one million. It exploded from one million to eight million in the next 90,000 years (from 100,000 to 10,000 years ago). Around 10,000 years ago, the earth had a large, better equipped human population.

By then, the last Ice Age came to an end; snow melted, and water reached the oceans. Gradually, the sea level increased to reach the present level. Increased water in the sea submerged major coastal grasslands and forests. This increased the density of human population. People killed more animals. As a result, the population of animals decreased. Palaeontological evidence proves that around fifty species of animals became extinct during that period. Men must have eaten up the entire population of these animals.

Anthropologists have concluded that around ten thousand years ago, food resources for the increased human population became insufficient. Gradually, many groups faced starvation: mankind reached the verge of extinction. Eminent historian Alfred Crosby says: 'Humankind was now faced with the choice of becoming either celibate or clever; predictably, the species chose the latter course.'

To understand the problem, it is mandatory to study the lifestyle of the people living 10,000 years ago. They lived a nomadic life as described earlier. Women collected vegetables from forests and men hunted animals. They usually did not go for hunting because of their involvement in pregnancy, lactation and infant care.

Women collected naturally grown food and thereby acquired good knowledge of the vegetation around them. Women were the caretakers of children, and therefore they required a secluded place to keep their children safe. Each mother had to make her own enclosure and spent most of her free time within it or its immediate surroundings. Hence, they tried to make their dwellings as livable as possible. Even today, the prime concern of most women is the creation of a secure, beautiful and cosy home around them.

During that period, the present institution of marriage did not exist. Males did not know their relationship with their children. They rarely cared about their night shelters. On the other hand, females lived with their children. Therefore, they came back to the night shelters by the evening. They along with their children formed the most primitive form of the human family.

To visualize the problem of food supply, consider an example of a nomadic band of the period. Abu Hureyra was a site of an ancient human settlement in western Mesopotamia. Here, archaeologists have excavated a settlement of a nomadic band that lived around ten thousand years ago. It consisted of a small number of round huts made of leaves and wood. The population of the settlement was more than two hundred. This was large enough to finish food from the adjoining forest. Consequently, they faced scarcity of food, especially in adverse weather conditions.

Try to imagine the challenges of the people living in Abu Hureyra. During each summer the grasslands of the place dried up. This compelled all herbivores to search for new grasslands, and carnivores followed them. The human band also faced scarcity of food. Priests and elders then planned to shift to a dense forest on the foothills. That forest was the ideal place to live during summer. Almost every year the band shifted to this place.

At the peak of one summer, all the people marched to the new forest. They reached the ruins of the huts they made the previous year. Soon, people began repairing their huts. One female of the group was in an advanced stage of pregnancy. She could reach the forest with difficulty. Other females repaired her hut first. While dusting, she found her mollusc-shell knife, corns, peanut shells and other articles. She cleaned the knife and threw out what she considered useless. That evening witnessed a storm followed by heavy rain.

Next day onwards, people began to search the forest daily. The pregnant woman was now too weak to go to the forest. She remained in her hut all the day. She took care of children of the band. Mothers of the children shared their food with her in the evening. Now, she sat at the door of her hut most of the time. A week after the rain, she saw greenery around the hut. She noticed a few small plants growing in the garbage heap.

Gradually, the band finished all the available food of the new forest too. Males explored the forest daily from morning till evening. They had already eaten most of the animals: usually they returned bare-handed. In the evening men discussed the whereabouts of animals with the priest. They asked what could be done to increase the number of animals in the forest.

Similarly, females also explored the forest daily but rarely found something to eat. In the evening, they gathered in the hut of the pregnant woman. They discussed the scarcity of edible plants. They began to imagine a forest full of edible plants only.

The pregnant woman was now confined to her hut and other women nursed her. One afternoon, she gave birth to a baby. Now, she rarely moved out for another month. Gradually, she regained her strength. She came out of her hut and observed the plants around her hut. She was seeing the greenery almost after two months.

Soon, she noticed the garbage heap. There, the plants grew nearly to her height. She noticed several baby corns budding on those plants. She recollected that two months ago she had thrown corns on this spot. She cried, 'I have discovered a way to grow a corn plant. Now, forests will only have edible plants.'

In fact, one cannot understand nature simply by wandering in a forest. To unveil nature, one has to sit patiently in its lap. Females watched nature patiently. They already had the knowledge of good cereals. Soon, they began sowing the seeds of cereals in the fields near their settlement. Now, they had no need to wander for food. Gradually, they modified their temporary huts into permanent ones. This simple discovery saved the human race from extinction.

From Abu Hureyra, archaeologists have excavated another human settlement. Excavations of this place show the earliest known evidence of agriculture. People of this band adopted cultivation for the first time on the earth. Abu Hureyra is an exceptional site where both nomadic and farmers' settlements have been excavated. Population of farmers was around ten times larger than that of the nomadic band. They lived in permanent houses made of mud bricks. The second group of farmers lived around five hundred years after the nomadic band. In fact, subsequent generations of the nomadic band formed farmers' settlement.

Anthropologists believe that agriculture was discovered accidentally in many places of the world. The example mentioned above is a narrative to depict how human beings could have invented cultivation. Eminent archaeologists Mithen Steven believes that global warming may have played a role in the development of agriculture, but it was not the crossing of a threshold in botanical knowledge.

There are many reasons to believe that females discovered farming. They were involved in collecting vegetables from forests and thus had a good knowledge of vegetation. Females suffered more from the scarcity of food. Their immobility before and after childbirth provided them with the opportunity to watch the growth of vegetation. Childbirth and childcare were facilitated by a sedentary life that was only possible with cultivation. Besides, many ancient myths propagate that some or the other goddess invented cultivation.

Invention of agriculture was a great scientific discovery that literally changed the face of the earth. A tiny seed grows into a plant which produces many similar seeds. This had been going on for ages, but it took thousands of years to be noticed. No other animal on the earth has learnt cultivation till date.

By the time calendars were invented, people all over the globe had adopted agriculture. Eminent anthropologist Mark Cohen says: 'Around ten thousand years ago almost everybody lived exclusively on wild food; by two thousand years ago most people were farmers.

Such a transition was indisputably the most important event ever engineered by the human mind.'

Agriculture changed the lifestyle of human being altogether. They no longer needed to look at the forests for food. Now, they had to stay near their farming land. Their permanent stay helped them to build better houses. Not only houses, men invented many useful techniques such as pottery, metallurgy, weaving, etc.

For early farmers, rain was the only way of irrigation. Without rainwater crops could not grow. At the same time, excess rain spoiled the crop through floods. Rain was variable every year and so was the production of crops. Gradually, yield of the crop became a major concern for the farmers. Priests in the farming community invented new gods to wrestle with the new problem.

Initially, priests of farmers advised worship of a mother goddess. In fact, the invention of agriculture gave rise to a fertility cult all over the globe. People worshipped female deities before agriculture too. During that time, people worshipped her ability to produce children. Priests observed that soil or earth produced plants and grains similar to a female body. They found no better symbol than a female to represent the earth. Therefore, the priests advised the worship of female idols. They assumed that the goddess blessed fertility and crops. They propagated that the worship of the goddess increased the fertility of the soil.

Almost every independent agrarian society developed its own goddess. The myths that glorified the role of the fertility goddesses were almost similar in every ancient society. During ancient times, artists of many places in the world carved statues of mother goddesses. These statues depicted a woman exhibiting her physical power and foodgrains. These mother goddesses remained the most powerful god for centuries. They had different names, such as Ishtar in Mesopotamia, Prithvi in India, Demeter in Greece and Isis in Egypt.

Ancient Greek priests advised worship of goddess Demeter. They proclaimed that goddess Demeter had invented cultivation. She taught farming and differentiated men from other animals. Initially, she was worshipped as a grain goddess and later as a goddess of childbirth and health as well. Greeks celebrated the festival of Haloa in the month of December to propitiate her.

Greek goddess Demeter

Egyptian priests began worship of goddess Isis around five thousand years ago. Initially, she was believed to cause the flood of the Nile. Later, she was worshipped to increase the fertility of both the earth and women. Gradually, worship of Isis became popular in the surrounding areas as well. Several temples dedicated to Isis were built in Egypt, Rome and Nubia.

Mesopotamians began worship of goddess Ishtar around five thousand years ago. She made the earth fertile and blessed farmers with a good crop. She was the daughter of the sky god. She was goddess of love, sex and fertility of the human race as well. Indians

Ancient depiction of Egyptian goddess Isis (1360 BCE)

also initiated worship of mother goddesses after they began cultivation. The Rig Veda mentions goddess Prithvi to represent fertility of soil. Gradually, all over India, idols and temples of many goddesses were built. Hindus still worship these goddesses.

Ancient depiction of Mesopotamian goddess Ishtar

Agricultural tribes of America worshipped a goddess called Cornmother. People believed that she gave birth to maize. Corn-mother discovered cultivation and gave the seeds to her husband. She blessed the soil with fertility.

Similarly, Indonesians worshipped Rice-mother. They believed that her body produced the crop of rice. She was also the guardian of crop and good fortune. The last sheaf of each crop was ritually cut and dressed as a woman. This sheaf was considered to contain the concentrated soul of the plants, the seed. In ancient Europe, the last sheaves of crops were designated as Wheat-mother, Barley-mother, and so on. Similarly, people of many places ritually preserved the last sheaf of each crop.

After discovering agriculture, men initiated a search for fertile plains in river valleys. They prepared farming lands by cutting or burning trees in the forests. Now, men had to stay at the same place, it was mandatory to grow crops in the same field every year. After men settled down, they domesticated animals such as the dog, horse, cow, buffalo, goat, etc. Men used these animals for riding, ploughing and milking. Gradually, small human settlements increased in size to become villages, towns, and ultimately cities. Thus, women turned the wanderer and the wild one into a domestic. They laid the foundation of homes, villages, cities and civilizations.

After the invention of agriculture, mankind continued its research. Priests of the farmers invented various scientific 'facts' and many gods. They noticed that one type of seeds germinate during a particular weather. The priests invented calendars to calculate the time of sowing. They studied the human body too.

The priests knew that men have continuous sexual desire round the year unlike animals that only mated during a particular season. Each male-female pair mated hundreds of times in a year. Females conceived after a spell of two to three years. Therefore, there was no obvious correlation of sex and pregnancy: neither the male nor the female knew that sex caused pregnancy.

However, after domestication, priests of farmers got the

opportunity to study pets. At that point in time, men must have understood the role played by a male in childbirth. It is likely that this discovery must have been made by ancient priests since they were the scientists of the period. They observed that most animals had seasonal sex: that is once a year or so. After each sexual act, the female animal became pregnant. Only after observing the domestic animals, priests could have learnt that pregnancy is an outcome of sex. Thus, animals must have taught basic biology to men.

After correlating sex and pregnancy, the priests concluded that the male had a certain role in childbirth. Some inquisitive priest must have explored the male's role in childbirth further. The priest experienced that the sexual act ends with release of some fluid from the phallus. What was the role of this fluid? Was this the seed of the child?

To dig out the truth, that priest must have tried sex without ejaculation of his semen for months together. He observed that this kind of sex did not impregnate his partner. Thus, the priest discovered that the ejaculated fluid from the phallus sows the seed of a child in its mother's womb. This kind of years-long researches must have established the male's role in childbirth. This discovery was no less significant than the knowledge of gravity.

With the help of this discovery, the priests gave birth to a new god. For a long period, men used to worship mother goddess because of her exceptional fertility power. Now, it was proved that she could not give birth to a new life alone. The priests were astonished by the role of males in childbirths.

The phallus sows the seed of a new life. The birth of new life! Well, the phallus was doing the job god was supposed to do! The priests already knew that the fertility of land was a result of rain – the shower of the sky god's blessing. Similarly, the shower of the phallus blessed the female with fertility. After this discovery, priests recommended phallus worship. Now, the fertility goddess was not alone; she was accompanied by phallic symbols.

All over the globe, there is enough evidence of phallus worship. The earliest evidence of phallic worship is various menhirs found all over the world. Menhir was usually a large stone that was set vertically into the ground that represented phallus. Anthropologists believe that after the adoption of agriculture, almost all farmer groups developed their own fertility cult, which comprised worship of one male and one female deity.

Regarding the discovery of male's role in reproduction, eminent archaeologist Peter Watson wrote, 'Given the fact that, in the very earliest times, the fertility of women must have been the greatest mystery and greatest miracle known to mankind, before the male function was discovered, and given the fact that menhirs almost by definition resemble the male organ, it is certainly possible that the megalithic cromlechs were observatories/temples celebrating man's new found understanding.'

Not only menhirs, gradually, people began to worship male idols. Commonly, these idols depicted a male with prominent genitals. At places, men worshipped stone idols of the phallus. For example, four thousand years ago, Egyptians worshipped Min. He was a masculine god of fertility, harvest and power. Min was portrayed as a man with an erect phallus.

Greeks worshipped Priapus as the god of fertility of men, cattle and vegetation. He was the son of Aphrodite, the goddess of love and wine. Priapus was depicted as a man with a big phallus. Priapus was known for his permanent erection, which gave rise to the medical term priapism.

The people of Athens, before the rise of Christianity, worshipped stone phalluses of Priapus. They offered flowers, fruits, milk and other food to the god of fertility.

Hindus have been worshipping the Lingam, a stone carved in the shape of a phallus, for centuries. Initially, the Lingam was a symbolic representation of the sky god Indra. Today, it represents Shiva, the

| Egyptian god Min | Greek god Priapus |

supreme god of Hindus. Other examples of phallus worship are Dionysian processions in Greece and Rome, Danube in Europe and the bull in the Indus Valley.

In fact, mankind experimented with everything possible in order to propitiate their imaginary gods. The next chapter will discuss the invention that changed the destiny of mankind.

4

Learning to Write

After adopting agriculture, men could grow enough food. Besides, they invented many utilities to lead a comfortable life. For example, they began spinning, weaving, shoemaking, grinding, making iron tools, etc. Usually, skilled people manufactured and sold these articles. Initially, the manufacturers bartered these for agricultural products. Later, coins of precious metals replaced the barter system. Gradually, cities became centres of manufacturing and selling.

As cities grew into trade centres, many farmers visited these cities regularly. Farmers came to the cities for treatment of their diseases too. These patients were treated by priests. Thus the business of priests also flourished in the cities.

Priests advised the kings and businessmen to build big temples. All the big ancient temples were built in the cities. Priests of these temples invented many new techniques of worship. Priests popularized their temples through magical stories. These temples and their priests also attracted farmers to the cities. Thus, around three to four thousand years ago, many cities became centres of trade and religion.

It has been discussed earlier that priests composed many short poems or hymns. Priests taught these poems to children. Around five thousand years ago, priests invented the art of writing. Earliest writing was developed by priests of four places: India, Mesopotamia, Egypt and China. The oldest writings of the world have been excavated from the Indus Valley in India. These were written around five thousand five hundred years ago. Around three thousand years ago, many cities of the world had developed writing.

Initially, to write, one diagram was drawn to express one thing, action or thought. Gradually, one diagram was dedicated to express one sound. The diagrams expressing sounds were called letters. Letters were designed for almost all the spoken sounds. A set of these letters was called an alphabet.

A complete set of the alphabet must have letters denoting all the sounds. It must have been a long and cumbersome job. It must have taken many generations. Making of the alphabet was not enough, the makers had to teach others to read and write it. Otherwise, only the alphabet makers could read their writing!

Ancient writings can be broadly divided into two categories. The first includes religious books such as the Rig Veda and the Bible. The other is excavated literature from river valley civilizations. The religious books were written on plant leaves and other unstable matter. Priests had to copy them almost every year. While copying they modified the original text and interpolated their own thoughts.

On the contrary, literature excavated from rivers valleys has a different kind of authenticity. These were written by priests on many tiles of wet clay with a reed or a bone. After writing, potters baked the tiles in fire. Thus, these writings on clay tablets were preserved unchanged for thousands of years.

No one could modify or interpolate the excavated texts. They describe the exact beliefs of the people. For example, the clay tablets excavated at Ras Shamra of Syria are considered more reliable as the source of the history of Babylonia than the Bible itself.

Apart from these, the excavated writings are far older than the religious books. The excavated literature was written by people who had recently adopted farming. Their near ancestors were nomadic. They must have continued to worship the gods of their nomadic ancestors. Therefore, the river valley literature can also guide us about the beliefs of the prehistoric nomadic people.

For example, let us consider Mesopotamia (modern Iraq), a fertile plain between two rivers, the Tigris and the Euphrates. The people living here founded the earliest civilization on the earth. Similar to all other ancient people, Mesopotamian civilization was also dominated by religion.

Huge numbers of clay tablets have been excavated from here. These are invaluable source material on evolution of religions. The beliefs of the Mesopotamians are further important since all the three monotheistic religions of the world find their roots in this sacred region. All the three have adopted many Mesopotamian myths.

The Mesopotamians were the first to construct a library. The library had thirty thousand clay tablets. These tablets mention the precise detail of their gods and the remedies for diseases. During prayers, people chanted flattering poems written on these tablets.

The most worshipped and powerful gods were Marduk the sun god and Ninurta the god of rain, thunder and storm. The poem 'Enuma Elish' refers to the sun as Marduk. 'Enuma Elish' was written in the third millennium BCE. The poem narrates the story of the creation of animals, plants and the earth. The poem has personified the sun, rain, the sky, etc. It mentions that the devil Tiamet fought a war against the lesser gods of Mesopotamia. In this war Marduk defeated Tiamet and made the heavens and the earth from her body.

Mesopotamian Sun God

Besides composing poems for the sun, the Mesopotamians made various ziggurats in the major cities. These ziggurats were built to worship the sun around five thousand years ago. Approximately twenty-five ziggurats are known today but almost all are in ruins.

The base of the ziggurats was a square raised platform of mud and bricks. Each side was around one hundred feet and its height was ten feet. Many platforms of reducing sizes were made over it to give the shape of a huge pyramid. These were stepping pyramids and had no internal chambers. Each ziggurat was the tallest building of its city. Usually, its height was around one hundred feet.

Mesopotamians celebrated the victory of Marduk over Tiamet at their New Year festival. They observed that the spring season caused trees to dry and shed old leaves. Soon, new leaves appeared to give a new life to the tree. They believed that all these new leaves were created by the sun.

The New Year festival Akitu was celebrated initially to mark the arrival of good weather and the sowing season. Later, it became an appropriate time for crowning a new king. The festival was celebrated at a special place near the temple. Priests recited the poem 'Enuma Elish' from the top of ziggurat.

This recitation from a height was an attempt to send their voice to the sun. Mesopotamian high-rise structures were not unique; people living at many places made similar structures. These revealed human desire to reach as near the sun and the sky gods as possible.

Egypt is the next site where ancient literature has been excavated. Again, a majority of writings is related to religion. Besides literature, Egypt had many graves, pyramids and mummies which helped in understanding the religious beliefs of the ancient Egyptians.

Excavations of Egypt meticulously portray the evolution of their gods and religions. In ancient Egypt, people worshipped hundreds of gods, and the sun was the first one. Around five thousand years ago, the city of Heliopolis was the centre of sun worship. The famous Sphinx also depicts the sun god. Many Egyptian kings, the Pharaohs, claimed to be descendants of the sun.

Around three thousand years ago, King Akhenaton with his wife Nefertiti introduced the concept that the sun is the only god. They believed the sun to be omnipresent and the sole creator of the universe. Akhenaton declared solar worship as the state religion of Egypt. Some scholars have credited Akhenaton to be the first monotheist.

Egyptian priests also composed flattering poems for the sun. People chanted these poems to worship the sun. One of the poems narrated: 'Men sleep like the dead; in the morning they lift their arms in praise, birds fly, fishes leap, plants bloom and work begins. The sun creates the child in the mother's womb, the seed in men and has generated all life. The sun has differentiated the animal species, their natures, tongues, and skins and fulfils all their needs.'

Egyptians believed that the sun had blessed them with the Nile River – the boon of Egypt. The sun blessed the rain. Nut was the name of the Egyptian goddess of the sky. Egyptians believed that

Egyptian Sun God

Nut swallowed the sun every evening and gave birth to it again each morning. Seth was the Egyptian god of rain and storms.

Archaeologists have found another evidence of solar worship from Tenochtitlán, an excavated city near Mexico. The city flourished around the time of Jesus Christ. It was the biggest city in America during its time, with an estimated population of two hundred thousand.

The citizens of Tenochtitlán made two pyramids for the worship of the sun and the moon. After the ziggurats and the great pyramids of Egypt, these are the largest and the most ancient man-made architectures in the world. The pyramid has a wide stairway that leads to the top. The top was used as an altar where human sacrifices were performed. During the sacrifice, masses stood below to watch the brutal procedure of pleasing the gods. They believed that the sun was watching the event from above.

Around these two pyramids many small pyramids were also built. After exploring a few of these, archaeologists were surprised. Each small pyramid had a human skeleton with bent knees and the hands tied at its back. These are enough evidence to conclude that each dead body was ritually sacrificed. Commonly, these human sacrifices were performed to revive the sun at the peak of winter. Their belief was confirmed every year; well after their human sacrifice, the sun gradually regained its strength!

It is now obvious that people of all the excavated river valley civilizations worshipped the sun and the sky gods. Not only excavated literature, historians have also found plenty of references of sun and sky worship in religious books. The following paragraphs narrate the prominent examples of such references found in the world.

Rig Veda – the sacred book of Hindus – is the most ancient surviving literature of the world. The book was written by ancient Indian priests. It has precisely narrated the sun, the sky and fire worship. It has many short flattering hymns for all the three gods. Hindus have been chanting these hymns for the last five thousand years. Historians believe that these hymns were composed millennia earlier.

In fact, Rig Veda describes the most ancient religion of the world. People worshipped the sun daily in the morning by chanting the Gayatri Mantra. During storms, floods and droughts, people worshiped Indra or Rudra, the sky god. Fire worship (yajna) was the central ritual of the people. To worship a god, people chanted short flattering hymns for that god. They worshipped their actual gods in the open and made no idol or temple. This religion will be discussed at length in the chapter on Hinduism.

Apart from this, the Jewish Bible, the Old Testament, also has portrayed God in the attribute of the sky god. This has already been mentioned in the Chapter 2. Ancient literature and the Bible attest that the age-old sky god metamorphosed into God. Several scholars believe that Jesus was personification of the sun; God was personification of the age-old sky god.

Iranian literature also mentions that people worshipped many nature gods before Zoroaster (sixth century BCE). Mithra the sun was their most important god. Even after Zoroaster, the cult persisted and spread into nearby civilizations like Rome. Around the birth of Christ, Romans worshiped only the sun. Many emperors of Rome encouraged solar worship during their time. Historians have found hundreds of inscriptions belonging to the second and the third centuries CE dedicated to the sun in the Roman Empire.

Before the dawn of Christianity, Romans celebrated 25 December as the birthday of Mithra the sun. Roman priests observed that the power of the sun reduced until 25 December. After this day, the sun became brighter every day. Therefore, Romans considered this day as the birthday of the sun.

The festival of Saturnalia was celebrated for seven days during this time of winter. Festivities began with a sacrifice at the temple of Saturn. People suspended their businesses and exchanged gifts. They celebrated this festival by lighting candles, feasting and drinking. Romans celebrated this time since they were confident about a bright future. They knew that the sun would burn brighter everyday after all the routine rituals.

Roman literature describes the end of the sun worship as well. The great emperor Constantine was a worshipper of the sun in his early life. The sun was supposed to be his companion. Constantine usually had a vision of the sun god in his dreams. During a battle, he is said to have had a peculiar dream. Jesus Christ appeared in his dream and advised him to inscribe the first two letters of his name on the shields of his troops.

The next day he saw another dream. He saw a cross on the sun with a caption below: 'This sign would give you victory.' Constantine won the battle. After the victory, Constantine perceived Jesus as his saviour and the messenger of the sun.

After the patronage of Christianity by Constantine in 312 CE, solar worship was consigned to oblivion. After adopting Christianity, Romans continued to celebrate 25 December, but as the birthday of prophet Jesus. Thus, the people living in the capital of Christianity worshipped the sun for a long period after Jesus. In fact, Romans initiated the worship of Jesus and God three hundred years after his death. French scholar Renan has said: 'If Christianity had been arrested in its growth by some mortal malady, today the world would have been worshipping the sun.'

Apart from these, Indo-European literature also portrays the sun as a symbol of divine power. The sun was the most popular deity among the masses. They depicted the sun as a disk on a chariot. Greek scriptures also describe worship of the sun that began in ancient time. They worshipped the sun regularly as the chief deity. The sun was believed to ride his golden chariot across the sky daily, while giving blessed light to everyone. In the evening, the sun sank into the western ocean and rose again in the east the next morning.

The ancient inhabitants of the Baltic region in eastern Europe practised the Baltic religion. The most important divinities in the Baltic religion were Saule (the sun), Meness (the moon), Dievs (the sky god), and Perkons (the thunderer). The Slavs of Russia also practised the worship of Perum (the thunder) and Svarag (the sun).

Literary evidence attests that Arabs, before Muhammad, worshipped the sky and the sun. In Japan, the sun goddess Amaterasu was considered to be the supreme ruler of the world. Even today, the sun symbol represents the Japanese state. They practise morning worship of the sun with breathing exercises. Susanoo the storm god was the younger brother of the sun goddess Amaterasu.

Besides religious literature, many historians have written the religious beliefs of their time. Around 2,500 years ago, Herodotus studied the religions of several different communities and found various similarities among them. He found that people usually worshipped the sun, the sky, the fire, the soul and their local gods.

These facts and logic again attest that the ancient world had only one religion. Well-organized religions of today came into vogue later. Ancestors of the Hindus, Buddhists, Jews, Christians and Muslims worshipped the sun and the sky before their religions were evolved. They developed similar methods of worship such as prayers, rituals, etc. Men perceived the sun and the sky as the almighty, creator, omnipresent and helpful. Modern gods of most religions also have similar attributes. The next chapter will discuss various methods invented by mankind to appease their gods.

5

Sacrifice: Bribing the Gods

The previous chapters narrated how men learnt many scientific lessons and how they created myths about the events they didn't understand. Around 5,000 years ago, farming gave rise to a few civilizations in different regions of the world. Within another 3,000 years, a majority of the earth's population switched to farming. Cultivation provided enough food to the people, but at the same time gave rise to many challenges. For example, their population exploded. Consequences of the increased human population are discussed at length in the next chapter.

Farmers faced another problem, that of droughts and floods. Nomadic people had the choice of shifting to another forest during scarcity of food. On the contrary, farmers could not move their settlements during droughts and floods as they had to cultivate the same land every year. Farmers discovered that seeds had to be sown in a particular season each year. They learnt the importance of rain for the crops. They had only limited artificial irrigation facilities. Farmers observed that every year the yield of the crop was different. They asked their priests how they could get a better crop.

Priests had already invented mother goddesses who blessed the soil with fertility. They advised worship of these mother goddesses to obtain good crops. They had also acquired the knowledge that the sky god governed rain and thunder. The sky god provided rain differently every year. Priests advised people to worship the sky god daily to obtain optimum rain.

Priests noticed that crops were dependent upon some other unseen forces of nature too. They advised some other rituals to appease these forces of nature. Priests of nomadic bands performed magic to hunt animals. Priests of farmers began to perform magic for crops. They devised many methods of worship, rituals and sacrifices to seek favourable weather for crops. Again, this was not a local concept; it was a global phenomenon. After the discovery of farming, all over the globe a new breed of priests appeared.

These priests of early farmers developed rituals to induce rain. The rituals comprised mimicries and prayers addressed to the sky god – the god of rain. For example, Tlaloc was the rain god of central Mexico. To seek rain, their priests took a ceremonial bath in a lake. During the bath, they imitated the cries of waterfowl and the croak of frogs. Mexican priests had heard frogs croak during the rains. Therefore, they believed that the call of frogs summoned the rain.

Similarly, Hindus also worshipped the sky god during droughts. Hindu priests sacrificed a male goat to the sky god. They usually performed this ritual on a cloudy day. Today also, there are temples where this ritual is performed every year, but now priests do a symbolic sacrifice. They incise one ear of a male goat.

Priests were clever enough to perform the rituals when rain was expected. Therefore, most of the time, rain followed the rituals. The onset of rain proved the efficacy of the rituals and the priest. Whenever there was no rain even after the ritual, priests put it down to some deficiency in the people's devotion. Besides, they repeated the ritual after a period and continued repeating it until the onset of rain.

Apart from such rituals, in order to control the forces of nature, priests advised performance of magic, hunting dances, rain dances and so on. Many tribal people still have a tradition of rain dance. For example, Cyprus is an island near Greece. Ancient people of Cyprus performed rain dance to induce rain. After the dance, people spat onto the back of a turtle, therefore they called it a spit turtle.

These rituals were done with the intention of obtaining the blessings of the sky god and other powers in the form of crops. Therefore, these rituals were performed before sowing or after reaping the harvests. While sowing, farmers asked for the blessing of gods; after reaping a good crop they thanked them. Gradually, the rituals performed after reaping took the shape of festivals. Today also, at many places of the world, festivals are celebrated after the reaping of harvest.

Gradually, priests flourished and became established professionals in all independently developing societies. They invented many useful superhuman powers. Priests were the professional hands behind the concept of gods. Priests invented rituals and gods; they composed and wrote the flattering hymns and they built and managed temples.

Now, the question arises how priests propitiated their gods? What kind of rituals did they initiate to seek the mercy of gods? All over the globe, priests invented one great technique to obtain blessings of their gods. Devotees of almost all religions have practised this since beginning. This great technique was sacrifice. The word sacrifice literally means to make something holy.

A sacrifice was a ritual in which some offerings were made to gods under the guidance of priests to please those gods. In other words, sacrifice was a kind of bribe to gods to seek their favour. Human killing was the earliest sacrifice that innocent men performed to please their gods. There is enough evidence of human sacrifices in history. Before people began to farm, they had no domestic animals, so human sacrifice was more common.

Anthropologists have found two distinct motives behind the practice of human killing. The first and the more common motive was to kill slaves or maids so that they might serve the kings' dead bodies in their afterlife. This does not seem to be a sacrifice to appease gods, but this was done in the period when kings were worshipped as gods.

Elaborate burial of kings were common in ancient Egypt. Although burial rituals began in the Stone Age, the ancient Egyptians practised the most elaborate burials. For Egyptians, life after death was a deep-rooted belief. They had a strong belief that the dead were still living and one day they might come back to life. They preserved the dead bodies of their kings through a long cumbersome process of mummification with several chemicals.

After death, Egyptian kings were mummified and buried with their worldly luxuries in the graves. The royal staff ensured that the body of their king had clothes, furniture, weapons and ornaments. They took special care to keep jars of wine along with food. Maids of his choice were killed, mummified and buried in the grave to serve the dead king. Egyptians believed that a maid could not serve the dead king as long as she was alive. Following this simple logic, the favourite maids of the dead king were killed and buried with the king in their official dresses.

The Egyptians built many pyramids to house the huge graves of kings. All these efforts were done to ensure that the dead king had a similar imperial life even after his death. Probably, the kings themselves planned their own burial rituals during their lifetime.

Another motive, behind killing a man, was to sacrifice him to some god. People sacrificed men within the temple and consumed the flesh of their body in a feast. This kind of behaviour defies logic today. There are many references to ritual human killing in archaeological, ethnographic and historical records. This was more common in the Stone Age when people had no domestic animal to sacrifice. Today, it appears that men must have killed and eaten their own people during scarcity of food. However, there was no evidence to suggest that ritual human killings were done by starving people. What were the reasons behind this brutal practice?

Anthropologists believe that people killed and ate their own tribesmen to acquire the power of their spirit. People believed that the flesh of the dead eaten by all the members strengthened the unity of the tribe. A few anthropologists hold a viewpoint that sacrificing life in a temple was an outcome of the belief in the immortality of the soul and its union with the gods.

Many tribes believed that human sacrifices provided strength to their god. Greek historian Herodotus and other ancient writers have described many human killers around the globe. In fact, human sacrifices were practised until medieval times, although rarely. In order to illustrate this most brutal practice of mankind, a historical example is narrated below.

Aztec was one of the Meso-American tribal groups; its members were well known for their bloody rituals. At the time of the Spanish invasion in the sixteenth century, the Aztecs frequently practised ritual sacrifice of men. Their priests performed bloody rituals in a horrible way to satisfy the sun. The Aztecs had a belief that the sun needed human blood and therefore they killed many people during each monthly ritual. This belief took thousands of lives each year.

The Aztecs believed that these sacrifices rejuvenated the sun annually. The rest of the year, they mutilated themselves to please their other gods. They believed that their gods had an insatiable thirst for blood. The priest pierced a finger, a tongue or an earlobe of a devotee to offer fresh blood to gods before each prayer.

The Aztecs selected either captured slaves or some warrior for the sacrifices. The ultimate honour for a warrior was either being killed while fighting an enemy or volunteering himself for the sacrifice. They also sacrificed children on certain occasions. The sacrificial victim was supposed to join the sun in heaven. The victim was housed and fed well until the time of sacrifice. He was honoured and respected as a god, since he was going to meet the god soon.

On the appointed day, all the priests worshipped the victim. Four muscled men immobilized him on the altar made on the top of a pyramid. The most experienced priest incised the victim's chest by an obsidian stone knife and reached the heart. He quickly dissected the heart out of the body while the victim was still struggling. The priest, with a victorious smile, exhibited the beating heart to the people standing below.

Once the body of the victim stopped moving, the priests pushed it from the top of the pyramid. Rolling down the stairs, the body reached the bottom, where another priest decapitated it. The head was kept on a stand inside the temple to honour the person.

Several other tribes around the globe also practised the ritual of cannibalism in one form or another. The Aztecs were dependent upon cultivation for food. They were aware of the value of human labour in food production. The most valuable commodity was obviously human life. Hence, they gifted the most valuable they had to their god. They killed their victims with the belief that the sun was watching and would bless them.

With the domestication of animals by farmers, the practice of ritual cannibalism was gradually replaced by animal sacrifice. Human sacrifice was reserved for certain occasions only. For example, the Incas sacrificed a man on the accession of a king, but on every full moon night they performed animal sacrifice.

At one point in time, human sacrifices were replaced with animal sacrifices. It was a logical modification of the ritual. People discovered a more convenient way to appease their god by sacrificing their domestic animals instead of their beloved ones. Initially, sacrifices by farmers were performed to seek a good crop and to protect themselves from diseases.

Besides praying for the fulfilment of their basic needs, they sacrificed animals to obtain luxuries such as wine, women and wealth. Sometimes, they practised this ritual to thank their gods. Again, sacrifice was not a local concept. At one point in time, people all over the globe sacrificed men or animals. Devotees of all ancient religions performed sacrifices in one form or the other.

For example, although flesh eating is prohibited today among many Hindus, they also practised animal sacrifice in ancient times. During the Vedic period, Hindu priests offered animals and other foods as sacrifice to their gods. The Buddha refuted all kinds of violence and therefore animal sacrifices as well. Under his influence, devotees of other gods like Vishnu and Shiva also stopped animal sacrifices; now they offered vegetarian food to their gods.

The basic ritual of Hindus was yajna, which involved the sacrifice of several food materials to the fire god. Hindus still continue to sacrifice whatever they think useful for them such as food, clothes and money. Priests of goddess Shakti continued sacrifices of animals despite the Buddhist influence and it is still practised in a few temples.

Ancient Jews are said to have had the tradition of offering their eldest son to God. They believed that childbirth reduced the energy of God, so they sacrificed children to rejuvenate God Yahweh! Gradually, Jews also adopted animal sacrifices instead of human.

For example, the Old Testament mentions that the childless Abraham, at the age of ninety, asked God to bless him with a son. God answered, 'Take me a heifer three years old, a goat three years old, a ram three years old, a turtle dove and a young pigeon.' Abraham collected the ordered menu and split each animal into two parts. Immediately, God promised a child to Abraham.

After many years, Abraham offered this blessed child Isaac as a sacrifice to God. God magically sent a ram for the sacrifice and saved Abraham's son. Later, Jews followed this very example of God and sacrificed their animals in place of their sons.

The ancient Chinese also practised human sacrifice and later replaced it with the sacrifice of domestic animals. Ancient Greeks sacrificed animals and consumed them in a celebratory meal to establish communion with gods. Ancient Roman also offered animals in sacrifice, accompanied by a prayer. Ancient Iranians worshipped Mithra the sun and sacrificed a bull for it in a ritual ceremony. Christians consider the death of Christ on the cross as a sacrifice. They believe it was the result of sins committed by humanity. Throughout the writings of St Paul, Christ is identified as a sacrificial victim.

The facts discussed above indicate that since time immemorial men have been killing men or animals. Why did men suppose that offering could please gods while it was obvious that none of their offerings reached gods? Men developed a notion that their devotion could make any god happy. How did this notion arise?

In fact, men had always conceived of gods similar to themselves. Whatever could make them happy was supposed to appease gods too. Priests advised people to offer the foods of their own choice to gods, propagating that this would please gods. However, all such offerings enriched only priests.

Anthropologists have suggested many theories regarding the origin of sacrifice. Commonly, they believe that sacrifice was the root of religion. For example, Sigmund Freud believed that the origin of religions and rituals is to be found in sacrifice. The British biblical scholar W Robertson Smith has also expressed a similar view: 'Sacrifices were motivated by the desire for communion between members of a primitive group and their god.' Almost all anthropologists agree that sacrifice was at the core of religious activity in ancient times.

Sacrifices were performed for one more specific reason. People had a conviction that sacrifices revitalized their gods. Why did ancient people nurture the idea that the almighty gods required human or animal life to revitalize them? This idea, to a certain extent, had its roots in the annual cycle of the sun.

In fact, priests observed that the changes of weather had a certain rhythm. At times, solar heat increased daily and one day it reached a peak. After this hottest day, solar heat reduced daily, and one day it reached the ebb. After this coldest day, solar heat began to increase daily to reach its peak again. This cycle was a rule of nature.

Ancient people lived in a colder weather. Reduction of solar heat perplexed and worried them. As per their instinct they began worship and sacrifice to revive the sun. The most common time for solar sacrifices was the shortest and coldest day of the year. After this day, brightness of the sun gradually increased every day. The revival of the sun after this day was a rule of nature. People perceived that the sacrifice had recharged the energy of the sun.

Other than solar revival, rain was another prime motive behind these sacrifices. Sacrifices to the sky god were made just before the expected rain. Usually, it began to rain within a few days after the sacrifice. If the sacrifice was not followed by rain, the priests repeated the sacrifice every week until it rained.

Human and animal sacrifices had some relation with the concept of the union of the soul with the divine. Priests had already invented the idea that every animal had a soul, which kept its body alive and left the body at the time of death. The soul was the spark that gave life to a physical body. The soul was considered to be an extension of the divine. Once the soul was free, it was believed to unite with its divine source. In fact, priests sacrificed someone and sent his soul to gods.

For example, Aztec priests believed that the soul of their victim would plead for them in front of sun god. Try to imagine the

SACRIFICE: BRIBING THE GODS ⁊ 63

thought process of many a priest after a sacrifice. First, the priest slaughtered the animal of sacrifice. He believed that soon the soul of the sacrificial animal would reach its divine source (some god) in the sky. There, the god and angels would inquire from that soul about the world. The soul would reply that the priest who slaughtered him was a great worshiper; the priest sacrificed him for the god. Thus, through the sacrifice, the priest transmitted an eyewitness account of his devotion to his god! It appears that many priests sent the soul of victims to their gods as a message that someone was asking for his mercy!

One irony, however, persists regarding sacrifices. People killed someone to please their kind gods! How could anyone conceive that the killing of an innocent being can appease a god, one who was supposed to be kind? How could someone who is kind be happy about a killing? First, let's consider, what would gods have achieved by the killing. Did gods eat the flesh of the victim? Did gods wish to see such a killing sport being simultaneously performed by men all over the globe? Did gods have some enmity with the animals being sacrificed? Quite unlikely, because no one had actually been in communion with any god.

People killed these animals only to eat them. People fooled even their gods and killed innocents in gods' name. Sacrifices were performed merely to satisfy human needs. Earlier, sacrifices involved killing a fellow man, a few harmless animals or birds such as a goat, a bull or a pigeon. Priests never tried to sacrifice a tiger! Later, sacrifice included only some material donation to the gods. In fact, priests obtained food, money and other necessities through these sacrifices. This can be understood through a study of the jobs of the priests of ancient times.

Ancient priests performed rituals to facilitate the growing of crops. They treated the diseases of farmers and their cattle. They performed rituals at the time of birth, marriage and death. They observed stars, planets, the moon, the sun, etc. They maintained calendars and gave advice about the favourable time to sow crops and to begin any new venture. Thus, they spent most of their time serving the community.

Despite all their services, the priests could not procure their service charges as the divine job of priests was considered to be a charity. Besides, they did not have their own fields and crops. They desired a share of the crops for their livelihood. No one shared his crop readily: the priests devised sacrifices to procure their share.

All over the globe, ancient priests adopted almost similar procedure of sacrifice. Firstly, the priests propagated the so-called benefits of sacrifices. For example, they proclaimed that sacrifice of a share of crops would provide a good crop in future. Sacrifice of food and clothes would bless a couple with a son. Sacrifice of a cow could cure a chronic patient. Such proclamations attracted people towards sacrifice.

Whenever, someone approached a priest for some blessing, he was asked to provide a specific item of sacrifice. Soon, the person reached the priest with the item. The priest chanted prayers, then took the sacrificed item, and kept it near the idol or the altar. After this, he chanted some hymn requesting the god to kindly accept that person's sacrifice and fulfil his wish.

Soon, the priest declared that gods have accepted the person's sacrifice. No god ever came to collect that sacrifice. Obviously, the priest took the item to his house. In fact, the priests started asking newer and newer sacrifices to earn their livelihood.

Other than sacrifices, priests devised methods to achieve a state of trance to propitiate the gods. Eminent sociologist Erika Bourguignon has written that to achieve an altered state of consciousness, which she generally referred to as trance, was a part of religious practices in 90 per cent of societies around the world. Priests believed that they could unite with the divine during trances.

Priests tried to induce trances through several forms of deprivation of basic instincts such as sex, food, water or sleep. The Buddha also tried all these deprivations to achieve enlightenment. Other priests tried intoxication, isolation from society, singing, dancing and chanting flattering songs. For example, Vedic people frequently ingested a drug called soma to achieve divine experiences. People believed that during intoxication they united with their gods.

To induce trances through musical prayers is still popular. Among Hindus, musical chanting of prayers serves the purpose of induction of trances. Today, many Hindu devotees claim that they had some divine experience during singing or listening to prayers. Truly, they have different experiences, but these are trances. These are the result of mental relaxation after listening to soothing musical beats. Besides, they believe that by singing the glory of their god they can unite with the divine. Faith and relaxation together hypnotize the devotee.

Other than prayers, priests invented another idea to appease their gods: fasting. Complete or partial abstinence from food, drink or both for ritualistic purpose is called fasting. Fasting for a specific duration in some special periods is practised in almost all major religions of the world. Fasting was a modification of the idea of sacrifice. Fasting for a day or a month was believed to propitiate god. Many pious devotees are seen to fast in order to achieve trances. Fasting was a common practice for priests to prepare themselves to approach gods.

Among major religions, only Zoroastrianism prohibits fasting. Jains believe that fasting and meditation lead to a transcendental state. Buddhists also observed ritual fasting on certain holy days. A devout Hindu fasts on many occasions. Both Jews and Christians fast during certain periods.

Since time immemorial, mankind has been practising sacrifices, rituals, prayers, devotions and fasting to appease their gods to seek their favours. Today, service to mankind is considered the best kind of worship. Many hospitals, schools and other charitable institutions have been established to serve humanity.

From the above discussion, it is obvious that ritual cannibalism of the Stone Age was replaced by sacrifice of animals. Later, sacrifices were replaced by fasting to suit people's comfort. Besides, people expressed their devotion through flattery. Later, wise men established that love and service to humanity are the best way to appease gods. These stages of worship from ritual cannibalism to the service of mankind were the stepping stones for human development.

6

Gods and Demons of Diseases

The earlier chapters narrated how people learnt about the powers of nature that influenced them. They began worshipping those powers as gods. Men worshipped everything from the sun to the phallus. Mankind wasted loads of working hours singing the glory of its gods. They killed domestic animals and even their fellow men brutally, to please their gods.

Gradually, men observed that there were certain events, which were not explained by any visible power. Men imagined that some invisible powers existed behind those events. What were those events? Why did our ancestors quest tirelessly for some unseen gods? Why did men persistently make efforts to please those gods?

The major reason behind men's quest for unseen gods was the horrible diseases they suffered from. How did human illnesses give rise to the concept of unseen gods? To understand this quest it is necessary to study the diseases that afflicted the ancient people and the remedies they used to cure them.

Since time immemorial, mankind has been suffering from some ailment or the other. Different diseases surfaced during different ages. For example, prehistoric nomadic men, before learning cultivation, did not suffer diseases prevalent today. They were frequently injured by wild animals. Their excavated dead bodies show no evidence of infectious illnesses such as cholera, plague or tuberculosis. Obviously, nomads led a healthier life.

The illnesses and remedies of nomads can be visualized through a study of the person treating them – their doctor. In fact, priests of nomadic people were working both as priests and doctors. A few decades ago, similar priest-doctors existed among many surviving tribes too.

These priests believed that diseases were either caused by magic cast by some enemy or violation of some tribal taboo. Priests were supposed to possess divine powers to cure illnesses. Their dress, cap and gestures were similar to magicians. They usually enjoyed special status and performed the roles of priests, healers and scientists.

These priests treated their patients through care, magic and herbal drugs. They treated common diseases like cough and cold through herbal medicines accompanied with diet restriction. Different kinds of magic were used to cure serious illnesses. Mental diseases were supposed to be caused by the possession of some evil spirit. Commonly, priests beat the spirit through the patient's body until it left him.

One example can explain the method of treatment of nomadic priests. Imagine a nomadic group of about a hundred people that lived some seven thousand years ago. One day, an adolescent boy among them suffers an epileptic fit. After that, he remains calm but confused. A few days later, during a fight with a peer, he suddenly develops violent tendencies. He starts abusing and shouting incoherently.

The priest of the group observes him; the boy is seen as if talking to somebody even when alone. The priest tries all the drugs and magic he knows and inflicts all the tortures he can on the boy. Despite the efforts of the priest, the behaviour of the boy remains unchanged.

One day, the boy has a fight with a peer, and he beats him to death. Now, all his peers are scared of him. The priest concludes that some demon has entered the head of the boy. The boy becomes a problem to the group. After days of thinking, the priest invents a surgical remedy to make a way out for the demon.

The priest advises drilling a hole in the boy's head to make a way out for the spirit. This is not a simple surgery. First, the boy is immobilized by at least four strong men. After that, the priest drills his head with a stone chisel and a hammer. Death is almost inevitable after such a surgery. Thus, the priest effectively kills the demon as well as the patient!

Many a human skull with a hole has been excavated in Peru, India, Britain, France and other parts of Europe. These people lived around eight thousand years ago and later. This procedure of skull trepanning was a treatment of a serious psychiatric illness like schizophrenia. A few of these skulls showed partial healing, which proves that they survived the surgery. The remedy was more painful than the disease itself. Some people practised skull trepanning to treat psychiatric illnesses even until the twentieth century.

It is surprising that priests made no effort to find out the route of entry of the evil spirit. Since the spirit had entered intentionally to live inside the skull, why would it leave even if a safe outlet was provided to it? Possibly, priests were not that ignorant; they just wished to kill the antisocial element.

The medical practices discussed above continued even after the invention of cultivation. As discussed earlier, around five thousand years ago, nomadic bands at many places of the globe adopted farming. This radically changed men's lifestyle. For example, cultivation necessitated a sedentary lifestyle instead of wandering. Now, farmers had sufficient food to eat. They had to stay near their farming land, which encouraged them to make better permanent houses. These protected men from wild animals and adverse weather.

Now, mothers and infants could afford good food and shelter. All these factors together paved the way for another population explosion.

Impact of this change can be visualized through one example. Imagine a nomadic group of two hundred people in the region of Egypt around five thousand years ago. The group discovered cultivation, settled in the fertile plains of the Nile and set up a village. The members of the group increased manifold in the next one hundred years.

Now, almost all the members of the group had permanent huts, clothes and food. The village became large enough to be called a town. This town already had one lake for their water-related needs. The lake was regularly filled by a natural spring round the year. The spring almost dried up in summer every year, but the lake fulfilled their daily need of water. Archaeologists have excavated many such towns with a population of more than ten thousand in Mesopotamia, Egypt and India. These towns flourished around five thousand years ago.

Suddenly, at the peak of one summer, this town faces a catastrophe: several people develop vomiting and diarrhoea. Gradually, they become weak, thirsty and restless. Their purging continues and some of them die on the second or third day of their illness. Meanwhile, some others also develop the same symptoms. It is not a personal illness but it has involved the whole community. People are facing such a mysterious illness for the first time after they settled. The suffering continues for a fortnight, but disappears gradually after the onset of rains.

Early farmers, all over the globe, faced similar epidemic or communicable diseases. These illnesses frightened the farmers. Anthropologists believe that epidemics attacked the human race four to five thousand years ago. Before that, the nomadic people never suffered this kind of illness. Eminent scientist Kenneth F Kiple has said that humans have been fighting the diseases of 'civilization' since they began congregating in large numbers. Then onwards, man is the most diseased animal on the earth.

Let's imagine the reaction of the people to this cholera-like illness. The horrible disease must have rendered the farmers sleepless with confusion and fear. Their priest was the only person familiar with the physical sufferings of the people. Obviously, anxious people would have turned to the priest to find an explanation and a remedy to this mysterious illness.

This priest of the farmers has been discussed earlier as well. He was not an ordinary person; his forefathers held the designation for ages. His ancestors briefed him about when, why and how they turned agriculturists. They precisely narrated many earlier mysterious deaths in the town. They taught him the remedies of common illnesses and injuries. He knew several stories of natural calamities such as lightning, flood, drought, earthquake and eclipses. He had acquired good experience of all burial rituals to protect people from ghosts. In spite of all his knowledge, he had never heard about such a disease that could involve many people simultaneously.

The new disease of diarrhoea posed an altogether new challenge to the learned priest. He advised some herbal medicines to the patients. But, the disease left the priest confused. How did the disease erupt? Who sent it? Why did only some people suffer? Why did only a few die? The priest recollected that all the dead patients excreted blood in their stool or vomitus during the last hours of their life. He concluded that some blood-thirsty power sent this illness. He advised sacrifice of some animal to quench the thirst of that power.

Anthropologists attest that sacrifice was a consistent ritual of all early farming societies. Animal sacrifice was common after the mysterious deaths caused by community illnesses. Later, priests initiated sacrifice of animals before the anticipated season of disease.

After a millennium, the population of the town mentioned above increased further and it grew into a small city. Now, the farmers had domesticated more animals. Although they had built good houses, these became more crowded. Let's try to visualize the diseases faced by the people living in the cities. For example, one Egyptian mummy, buried around four thousand years ago, had evidence of tuberculosis. Obviously, the mummy suffered the disease in her lifetime.

The suffering of the mummy from tuberculosis could be predicted precisely. One year before her death, she was leading a normal life. But then, she gradually developed typical symptoms of tuberculosis such as cough, loss of appetite and mild fever. The priest of the town prescribed all the medicines he knew for fever and cough for her. Within a month, she became pale and frail. Now, the priest tried various herbs with acrid taste to cast the demon of the disease away.

The priest had ample time to experiment on such patient. After two months, the patient developed severe back pain. Ultimately, the patient became bedridden and began coughing copious amounts of sputum. Now, it became difficult for the priest to answer as to why all his remedies had failed to respond. The patient continued to become weaker and paler, and ultimately died.

The priest was also left confused by the mysterious illness. He initiated some analysis – the post-mortem. He thought that the appearance of the patient was peculiar. She appeared pale, as if someone was sucking her blood. At the same time, there was no mark of injury on her body.

The intelligent priest tried to predict the culprit. Who could suck the blood of the patient without a cut in the skin? Only some divine power of god or demon could do such a job. Therefore, the priest blamed some demon. He explained that the soul of some dead person had been transformed into a demon, which sucked the patient's blood.

Again, this was not the thought of just one priest: it was a global theory. Many magical treatments such as amulets, potions and incantations were applied in cases of tuberculosis. In the medieval period, such demons were called vampires. It was believed that vampires sucked the blood of tubercular patients. This belief continued for a long period, even as late as the eighteenth century.

People believed that vampires lived in their graves. They came out of their graves to suck blood. Therefore, people made efforts to arrest them within their graves. From medieval to early modern period, many graves were exhumed to treat patients of tuberculosis. People dug the grave of the suspected vampire. After digging, they made serious efforts to confine the movement of the dead body. For this, they cut its head, tore its heart and nailed the rest of the body to the bed of the grave. Thus, the people left no stone unturned to arrest the vampire within its graves.

Around four thousand years ago, priests in cities developed the skill of writing. Then onwards, they wrote down their medical knowledge and practices. The earliest medical literature of the world was written on clay tablets in Mesopotamia. Their priests noticed a set of symptoms, named it, imagined its cause and suggested some ritual as its cure. For example, a typical tablet mentions: 'The patient with X symptoms, suffers from disease Y, caused by demon Z; do ritual of god A to cure.'

Some tablets describe that diseases were caused by entry of invisible demons into the human body. The priests performed rituals to irritate the demon, who they believed had caused the diseases. Ritual remedies included potions, prayers, incantations, sacrifices, etc. The potions were usually mixtures of disgusting ingredients to nauseate or irritate demons. People believed that the bad taste of mixtures compelled the demons to leave the patients.

Not only magic, Mesopotamian priests developed some scientific remedies too. They used herbal drugs, plasters and suppositories.

They applied honey on wounds and sores. Today, honey is known for its antiseptic properties. They used sulphur for common skin troubles, including scabies. Sulphur is a proven remedy for skin diseases. They also developed remedies for dyeing grey hairs, toothache and bad breath. A tablet inscription of the early second millennium BCE reads: 'Do not use a pot used by a patient.' This proves that by that time Mesopotamian priests had learnt the danger of infections.

Around four thousand years ago, Mesopotamian priests began to worship the wine goddess and used wine as a medicine. Alcohol was the first drug men learnt to synthesize. This was another great accidental invention after agriculture. It is difficult to say whether men began to use alcohol for fun or medicine. Alcohol was the only man-made antimicrobial with the early farmers. Only fifty years ago, many tribal people used home-made brew as the remedy for almost all ailments. As an antiseptic application, it is widely and effectively used in modern medicine as well.

Mesopotamians also practised surgery, but rarely, because it was a risky job. One of the tablets mentions: 'While operating on the eye of a patient, if the surgeon killed the patient or damaged the eye, his hands would be amputated. If the patient was a slave, the surgeon would serve as a slave to the old master.'

Ancient Egyptian writings also mention that magic had an important role in the cause and treatment of diseases. Around four thousand years ago, a priest-doctor called Imhotep wrote a book of medicine. Later, Imhotep was designated as the Egyptian god of medicine, and he was worshipped for a long period. His book mentions examination, diagnosis, treatment and even prognosis of different diseases.

The book mentions many incantations and a list of foul substances to cast away the demons of diseases. For example, it advised a special mixture of irritant herbs for patients suffering with abdominal problems. After drinking the mixture, the patient usually complained of bloating and pain. This was supposed to be an indication that the drug was fighting with the demon inside. After some time, either the drug killed the demon and cured the patient or the demon killed the patient!

The Indian system of medicine originated around five thousand years ago. It was first written in the Atharva Veda. Indians also practised magic to expel the demons supposed to cause diseases. The ancient Indian god of medicine was Indra – the sky god. Indians used many effective herbal medicines too.

Greeks also believed that demonic possession caused diseases. Their priests treated patients by magic and faith healing in temples. Greeks regarded dreams as divine. Their god of healing was Asclepius, and they made many temples dedicated to him.

Patients were ritually prepared before entering the temple for treatment. These temples were filled with holy snakes. The patients had to sleep in the temple. Their priests believed that after sleeping Asclepius visited the temple and the holy snakes licked the patients to cure. Today, the emblem of allopathic medicine depicts two snakes. In fact, the emblem was drawn in ancient time to depict the healer snakes of the Greek temples.

Medical practices in ancient Israel were written in the Jewish Bible, the Old Testament. This book also mentions that the diseases were caused by God and demons. For example, the book describes diagnosis and treatment for leprosy. Whenever a person developed rashes on his skin, he had to consult the local priest who examined the skin lesions. If the priest identified typical rashes of leprosy, the patient was declared unclean and possessed. Each new patient, thus labelled unclean, had to live outside his city with other lepers. To visit the city, he must have a valid reason. During the visit, it was mandatory for him to cover his mouth and to shout 'Unclean, Unclean' all the way.

The priest visited the lepers' camp every seventh day to observe the healing of lepers. Weeks later, the patients who showed signs of healing were selected for treatment. The priest advised each of them to catch two birds. The patient was advised to kill one bird over a water vessel and mix its blood into the water. After this, the patient had to bath in the water mixed with blood. The priest believed that the demon of leprosy had been washed into this water. The patient had to collect the water he bathed in and to rinse the other bird in the collected water. After the treatment, this innocent bird was allowed to fly with the demon of leprosy.

The patient bathed thoroughly on his arrival in the city again. The next day he had to bring three lambs for different rituals. The priest sacrificed all three lambs. He painted the right ear, thumb and big toe of the patient with their blood. The priest applied other holy liquids over different parts of the patient's body to make him 'clean' again.

Besides the medical practices mentioned above, ancient people indulged in other medical practices too. For example, priests chanted a charm, hymn or poem to control bleeding. For patients suffering from fever they cut the veins and released some blood. For all mental illnesses, they tortured the patient. Most ancient oral medicines had bitter taste as it was believed that the bitter taste would irritate the demons possessing the patients. Most of the local applicants were also irritants to the skin.

Thus, ancient books describe the magical practices invented by their authors. Surprisingly, many ancient books contain only religious and medical practices. In fact, these books were written by priests of farmers to relieve their sufferings such as diseases, droughts or floods. They wrote about their gods and the demons behind human suffering and their remedies such as prayers, rituals or sacrifices.

Despite the sincere efforts of priests, the diseases afflicting the farmers increased. After each new disease, priests of every locale stretched their imagination and invented a new god. Around three thousand years ago, people all over the world faced new diseases. They observed that their old gods could no longer help them, they initiated a quest for some more powerful gods.

Priests already knew the gods responsible for weather, droughts or floods. They could not find any obvious power behind the new diseases of the people. They visualized that some unseen god must have sent them. A few philosophers and priests named and described such unseen gods. By then, priests had learnt writing; therefore they wrote all their thoughts in the form of books. Gradually, the miserable masses began worshipping these new gods.

Decades after these writings, many priests propagated that the ancient books were dictated by the unseen gods. The authors just wrote what the gods dictated. The books written at that time are still the modern religious texts. These books gave birth to present-day gods and religions. This turn of history altogether changed human life. What were the new challenges faced by the people of that period?

Around three thousand years ago, people worshipped the sun, the sky, fire, mother goddesses and other local gods. By and large, they had adopted agriculture. The last Ice Age came to an end well before the start of agriculture, making the earth warmer. Initially, cultivation was adopted by the people living in the warmer areas of the earth.

Farmers now had houses, clothes and a fair control over fire, and all these reduced their dependence on sunlight. They regularly maintained hearths that made it easy to use fire. Gradually, fire became a common household entity and that degraded its divine image. Fire, clothes and houses reduced the necessity of the sun. All these factors together took the shine off both the sun and fire.

Priests were the scientists of that time; both prayers and magic were the discoveries of the period. By then, many philosophers also joined the priests to solve the new challenges faced by human beings. They both invented modern scientific knowledge too. They had already learnt to write, and now they developed counting and mathematics. They observed the sun persistently to predict favourable weather for sowing, which increased their knowledge of the sun. They observed that every day the sun reached its peak. They noticed that the time between two solar peaks was the same and they considered it an unit of time – a day.

They found that solar heat changed regularly. At times, they noticed that the duration of daytime reduced every day. Shorter daytime chilled the weather. Gradually, the shortest day came around, and then the solar heat began to increase every day. This prolonged the daytime and heated the atmosphere. Gradually, the longest day came, and then the solar heat began to decrease again.

Priests identified the shortest and the longest days. They found that the number of days between the two shortest or two longest days were the same. The period between two shortest days was a complete solar cycle, and they designated it another unit of time – a year. Priests of almost all ancient civilizations independently calculated nearly the same number of days in a year.

Priests also observed the lunar changes and found them to be consistent on every twenty-eighth day. Priests considered this as another unit of time – a month. Writing made it possible to note down the solar and lunar changes. This gave rise to calendars. Priests made calendars to guide farmers on the best time for sowing.

Priests observed other visible planets and infinite number of stars, and wondered about them. Other than stars, they identified seven movable celestial objects: the sun, moon, Mars, Mercury, Jupiter, Venus and Saturn. They dedicated one day to the worship of each object alternately; this led to the concept of the week. After regularly watching the sun and the moon for centuries, the priests concluded that both revolved around the earth consistently, as if obeying some other power.

Besides, in that period, men worshipped the sky god. They were scared of storms – the wrath of the sky god. Many incidents proved that the sky god could destroy men through rain and lightning. For farmers, floods and droughts were persistent nightmares. Floods destroyed their crops and houses. During droughts nothing could grow in their fields. On the contrary, optimum rains – the blessings of the sky god – made their crops flourish. Almost all civilizations continued to worship the sky god both as a saviour and a destroyer. Thus, the sky god remained as powerful as ever.

Knowledge of the sun and other celestial objects brought forth more questions than answers. The wiser generations began to explore the sky further. Why did the power of the sun decline? Why did its power increase again? Why did the weather change? How did droughts, floods and earthquakes happen? Who was behind the changes of the earth and its sky? Who was running all the celestial bodies? Why did not they collide?

Not only the movement of the celestial bodies, but their origin too was a mystery. How did the celestial bodies come into being? Who was the creator and the governor of all these? It was inconceivable that this immense universe was running without any controller. It was beyond their comprehension. There must be someone who rotated all these celestial objects without collision.

Priests could not imagine the gravitational force and the coherence of celestial bodies. They consoled themselves and the masses that some power had created the sun, moon, planets and stars. That power controlled their movements as well. Soon after this realization, the wise priests had many new questions. What was the name of the power? What was its location? How did it look? What gestures appeased or annoyed it?

Not only the sky, but some other events and objects of nature also confused priests and philosophers. What lay beyond the insurmountable barriers like the sea or the mountains? Why did flowers bloom and fruits ripen at a particular time of the year? The farmers sowed the seeds of the crops, but who sowed the seeds in the vast forests? Why did many plants die after fruiting? Why did the crop yield vary every year? Why did trees shed their leaves? How did new leaves appear after a period? Why did many insects appear at one particular time of the year?

After much study, priests and philosophers concluded that there was some harmony, cycle, coherence or coordination in all the changes of nature. The thought of coordination gave rise to another question. How could the speechless plants and animals coordinate? To explain this, the priests imagined some power that harmonized them. They visualized that seasons, plants and animals obeyed some unseen power. For example, around three thousand years ago, an Iranian priest Zoroaster had expressed similar thoughts in the book Avesta. He wrote:

> O Lord, reveal me the truth!
> Who was the father of the cosmic law?
> Who created darkness and sparked light?
> Who made dawn, midday and night?
> Who assigned orbits to the sun and the stars?
> Who caused the moon to wax and wane?
> Who held the earth and the sky?
> Who prevented them from falling down?
> Who maintained the waters and also plants?
> Who provided speed to winds and clouds?
> Who created the living beings?
> Who planned sleep and wakefulness?
> Who monitored the duties of man?
> Who other than Thee?
> This I wish to know!

To answer the questions mentioned above, Zoroaster imagined one almighty god Ahura Mazda. He preached that all the celestial bodies, weathers, plants and animals were governed by Ahura Mazda. Thus, Zoroaster gave a name to the imaginary power. Not only Zoroaster, but other contemporary priests of the globe also had similar questions and their answers.

For example, the Bible (Psalm 74: 12–17) mentions:

> Yet, O God, my king of old,
> Maker of deliverance throughout the world,
> You are the one, who smashed sea with your might,
> Cracked the heads of the Tannin (dragons) in the waters,
> You are the one, who crushed the heads of Leviathan (demon),
> Left him as food to the people,
> You are the one who broke open springs and streams,
> You are the one, who dried up the mighty Rivers,
> To You belongs the day, Yours too the night,
> You are the one, who established the light of the sun,
> You are the one who fixed all the boundaries of the world,
> Summer and winter—it was You who fashioned them.

Apart from these mysteries, people in that period faced many miseries as a result of their changed lifestyle. Around three thousand years ago and later, the world had several cities with populations exceeding fifty thousand. The citizens lived with domestic animals in small crowded houses with poor drainage systems. The drained water collected near the houses. Various blood-sucking insects like mosquitoes thrived in stagnant waters.

Permanent human settlements attracted pests as well, such as mice, rats and cats. They considered the cities as safe, cosy and rich places to live. Bigger social structures resulted in huge waste disposal around cities consistently. Houseflies and other vectors flourished in the piled garbage. These vectors carried the infections of garbage to human food. Moreover, people defecated in the open fields. Thus, the excreta of men and domestic animals contaminated drinking water. Amoebae, hookworms and other parasites excreted in animal faeces found a way to reach the intestine of men. Fleas and lice living on domestic animals found opportunities to cruise on human bodies.

Now, big families of farmers lived in small houses. Thus, all family members lived within spitting, coughing and sneezing distances from one another. Overcrowded men, pets, rodents and insects exchanged their diseases with each other. By then, the concept of personal hygiene such as daily bathing or brushing of teeth was not popular.

Without personal and public hygiene, almost everyone frequently suffered from viral, bacterial or malarial infections. Mortality of mothers and infants, during childbirth, was common. Since the placental cords of the newborns were incised with dirty knives, many infants died due to tetanus within a few days of their birth. Many mothers died during childbirth because of excessive bleeding and/or infection. But thanks to the immense fertility of men, their population flourished despite the adversities.

The farmers suffered from many new diseases, as if they had sown the seeds of diseases too! Around 2,500 years ago, the above-mentioned dirty and crowded cities encountered a new but most horrible community suffering called plague. Historians have written about many plague epidemics worldwide.

The plague of Athens was the earliest documented plague in history. Around 2,500 years ago, Athenians were waging a war against their neighbouring country Sparta. Therefore most people confined themselves within the city walls. People from the countryside also came to the city for security and thus crowded the place. Soon, the great plague epidemic broke out. Contemporary historian Thucydides himself suffered from this illness but survived to write:

All of a sudden, many healthy persons developed severe headache and fever without any obvious cause. Besides, they complained of sneezing, sore throat, cough and chest pain. The spells of cough gave a near-death experience to the patients. Their tongue became bloody and emitted a fetid smell. Their skin was hot, reddish and developed small eruptions. The patients could not wear clothes due to the burning skin lesions. Some of the patients were seen dipping themselves in water ponds. They suffered the miserable feeling of unrest and insomnia. Later, they coughed sputum mixed with blood. A few of them died on the fourth or fifth day. Around the eighth day, the surviving patients regained some strength. Now, some of them developed severe diarrhoea, which killed them. The rest survived with severe weakness. Each survivor had some permanent damage to one or the other organ or to their memory.

The plague of Athens killed almost one-third of its population. The enemy army fled after watching a view of several funeral pyres. The remaining people of Athens developed a fear that they too were soon going to die. They ceased to fear the law. People learnt that each new sufferer was in some way related to the previous patients. Therefore, they stopped caring for their family members. Patients were forced to live together in one common home. Once they died, the survivors did a mass cremation to protect themselves.

The frightened Athenians consulted their priests. The priests already believed that illnesses were caused by demons. They practised herbal and magical remedies. They tried some bitter herbs to cast away the demon of plague. What else could they do? Plague was an acute illness lasting around three to four days only. Therefore, the priests hardly had any time to do anything except beating about the bush.

The Athenian priests propagated that the god Apollo sent this horrible illness. Some logical people believed that the disease was caused by some smell in the air, so they began wearing a mask. A few women kept a bunch of flowers to protect themselves from the smell of the plague. Some people burnt spices like red chilli to irritate the demon and cast it away from their houses. Burning incense sticks for purification of temples, shops and houses is a consistent practice in almost all religions. This practice must have been initiated as an attempt to drive away the demons of infectious diseases.

Not only in Athens, during the last three thousand years many epidemics of plague have killed billions of people worldwide. The illness was so horrible that many people fled to nearby cities to protect themselves. Soon after reaching, a few of them developed the illness, and thus the disease spread in the new city. For a very long period, the disease killed many people and the survivors feared the worst.

Mankind could invent a cure for this disease only seventy years ago. It is surprising that man, the wisest animal on the earth, could not explore the cause of this illness for such a long period. In fact, the human race did not make concerted scientific efforts for two thousand years. Why didn't the scientists endeavour to wrestle with such a mass killer? This question can be answered by the religious texts.

Each episode of plague-like community illnesses left many curious survivors. For priests also, epidemics were an altogether new challenge, which had to be explained. The people suffered from similar symptoms. Therefore, the wise priests had to find a common cause. Similar to the Athenians, the only option left to priests was to blame some divine powers. The previous gods of farmers – the sun, the sky and fire – could influence them, but never killed them directly. Other gods such as mother goddesses influenced their crops, but they also did not punish the people with death.

Priests and philosophers were already visualizing one new god behind all the mysteries of nature. Now, they imagined that the new god must be capable of causing epidemic diseases like plague too. This god must have a magic weapon that could actually punish people by killing a major chunk of them simultaneously. This newly discovered god was the most powerful among all the previous gods, since his punishment was obvious.

All epidemic diseases had some correlation with rain and the weather. Droughts and floods were usually followed by epidemics. Rain was ultimately dependent upon the appearance of the sun and the sky god. Thus, priests supposed that the new god sent epidemics through the sun and the sky. This indicated that the sun and the sky also followed the same god. Obviously, this god must be responsible for the movements of all other smaller celestial objects too.

In fact, priests and philosophers imagined a god that was omnipresent and omnipotent. They believed that this new god created and nourished every creature. This god governed all the celestial bodies and the sky god. He was behind every mystery of nature. This new god was supposed to be the one ultimate power. Monotheism, the concept of one and only one God, emerged this way. Monotheism was an attempt to explain all the mysteries and miseries faced by mankind.

This one and only one God was named differently in many different geographical places. Priests invented many prayers and sacrifices to propitiate God. Not only priests, people worldwide were also convinced that God was sending diseases. This theory gave rise to many questions. Logically, an angry God would inflict the disease on everyone. Why was then God killing some people only? Priests wasted long hours to decipher this mystery. They stretched their imagination and tried to sort out the differences among people.

Priests observed that different people have different colours and shapes. They noticed that there was a vast difference in their behaviour and therefore priests tried to identify those acts of people which could annoy anybody. Obviously, those acts might annoy God too. What were those habits or acts? What kind of acts annoyed God? What kind of acts pleased God? Many people were doing antisocial activities that annoyed the rest of the people. Priests designated many habits or acts as offensive, antisocial or immoral – the sins. They concluded that these sins provoked the anger of God and He punished the sinners through diseases. Here, the notion of sins and good deeds entered the scene.

This theory achieved three objectives in one stroke. First, it explained that the diseases were the outcome of sins. Second, now priests had the whip of God – the plague – to control crime. Third, it explained the reason for fortunate non-sufferers from the plague. Although priests solved the puzzle of epidemic diseases, they arrested scientific understanding. In the darkness of such superstitions, people worshipped God and made no scientific efforts to find the reasons behind illnesses.

Again, this theory was not an individual thought but a global invention. To understand this invention, it is necessary to study the society of that time. Around three thousand years ago, the population and diversity of the cities were increasing. Tribal feelings were replaced by personal fortune. All ancient cities developed well-distinguished classes, depending on the wealth of individuals. In fact, slavery was also a result of civilization. For example, half the people of ancient Athens were slaves.

Class differences, jealousy and revenge gave rise to many crimes such as theft, quarrels, murders and rapes. The ancestors of these farmers were nomadic who had the instinct to collect and hunt. This behaviour persisted in many city dwellers; so they stole cattle or crops. Thus, the farmers living around three thousand years ago and later faced a big problem of crime.

Nomads lived in forests, so they required no social rule to follow. But, people living in a society required rules with punishment for violators. By this time, there were no powerful civil authorities. The people usually followed the commands of divine powers.

Throughout the world, priests themselves made moral rules and propagated that gods had dictated them. Violation of these divine rules was considered a crime or a sin that attracted divine punishment. Since gods would not use some weapon to punish the sinners, priests declared that gods punished the sinners through diseases and poverty.

Let us consider this theory in the light of documented historical facts. This theory of diseases was developed by the priests and philosophers of several places in the world. It was well documented in ancient religious books. For example, plagues were best described in the Jewish Bible, which was written around three thousand years ago or later.

According to the book, plagues were natural calamities killing a major chunk of the community. Calamities were either famines caused by floods and droughts, or epidemics such as tuberculosis, cholera, typhoid and plague. All these calamities were sent by God.

The book mentions that prophet Moses said that one day, he met God Yahweh. He declared that God Yahweh had sent ten plagues of the past. Moses further propagated that God had ordered the people to follow ten moral rules – the Ten Commandments. He warned the people that if anyone violated these rules, God Yahweh would inflict plague on him as punishment. The Ten Commandments are:

(1) I am the Lord your God, (2) Worship no other gods but me, (3) Do not use God's name falsely, (4) Keep the Sabbath day holy, (5) Respect your father and mother, (6) Do not kill, (7) Do not commit adultery, (8) Do not steal, (9) Do not tell lies about other people, (10) Do not envy other people's possessions.

Literature is the mirror of contemporary society. Similarly, the Bible narrates the thoughts of priests of the era. In fact, before the attack of plague, Egyptians worshipped the sun, the sky and local deities. Moses observed many deaths by plague, and soon he imagined some almighty power behind plague. That power was bigger than the sun and the sky god. In other words, the killer plague showed the glimpse of the one true God to Moses. At the same time, the ten rules of Moses provide an insight into the problems of the society of that time.

Moses was not a common priest but religious and political leader. Later, he was designated as a prophet. Gradually, many distant people and priests accepted the theory of Moses and the new religion – Judaism. After the birth of God, Jews consigned their older gods into oblivion.

Not only in Egypt and Israel, similar notions of the divine origins of diseases were invented at many places in the world. For example, in India, the Buddha (563–483 BCE) was perplexed with human sufferings. He initiated his quest for the cause and remedy of evils such as disease, debility and death. Death and debility as a result of ageing were the rules of nature. So the Buddha had to discover an answer to the diseases only. During meditation, he concentrated mainly on the cause and remedy of human illnesses.

His famous enlightenment was not some miraculous meeting with some god. It was the realization that human deeds or karma were the root of all human suffering. Good deeds were rewarded by bliss; bad deeds, sins by suffering. The Buddha declared that each human birth was a suffering spell. The world was like a torturing place like hell. People took birth as a punishment of their sins committed in previous births.

It was a great discovery of the time, and the ideology attracted a massive following. Several Buddhist books popularized the concept. For the next two millennia, almost half the population of the world believed and still continues to believe the concept propagated by the Buddha. In fact, the Buddha did not name the god who inflicted the punishment. After the Buddha, many Hindu texts also narrated the same story that diseases and poverty of the people were punishments for their sins.

In Iran, Zoroaster (628–551 BCE) was also concerned about the suffering of humanity. He conceived a god Ahura Mazda above the sun and the sky gods just to explain human miseries. In China, Lao-tzu in sixth century BCE and later Confucius were also perplexed with the sufferings of people through epidemics.

During the above period, men not only invented new gods, but also learnt many scientific lessons to prevent infectious diseases. For example, Jews must be credited for their invention of hygiene. Their Bible mentions many rules of sanitation. Jewish priests practised isolation of patients, washing after handling a dead body and burning garbage.

Hindus also made rules of sanitation. Washing hands many times was a basic teaching of Hinduism. Bathing before any worship or ritual was mandatory. Jain prophet Mahavira advised more strict rules of sanitation. Thus almost all religions made rules of hygiene a holy duty. Although the rules were propagated as gods' wish, these were the scientific ways of preventing diseases. Contemporary priests worked as municipal commissioners to implement the rules of sanitation in society.

These diseases were not restricted to the regions discussed above, but were the scourge of people throughout the world. It is not coincidental that almost all the philosophers of those ages worked on human anatomy and remedies of diseases. Greek philosopher Hippocrates was the first one to declare that diseases were natural events; gods or demons had nothing to do with them. Although Hippocrates began his career at the snake temple of Asclepius, he had a scientific bent of mind. For example, in those days, patients of epilepsy were invariably supposed to be possessed by an evil spirit. He argued that it was caused by some blockage in the brain.

Hippocrates wrote the first scientific medical text – some sixty books, six of which are believed to be his original work.

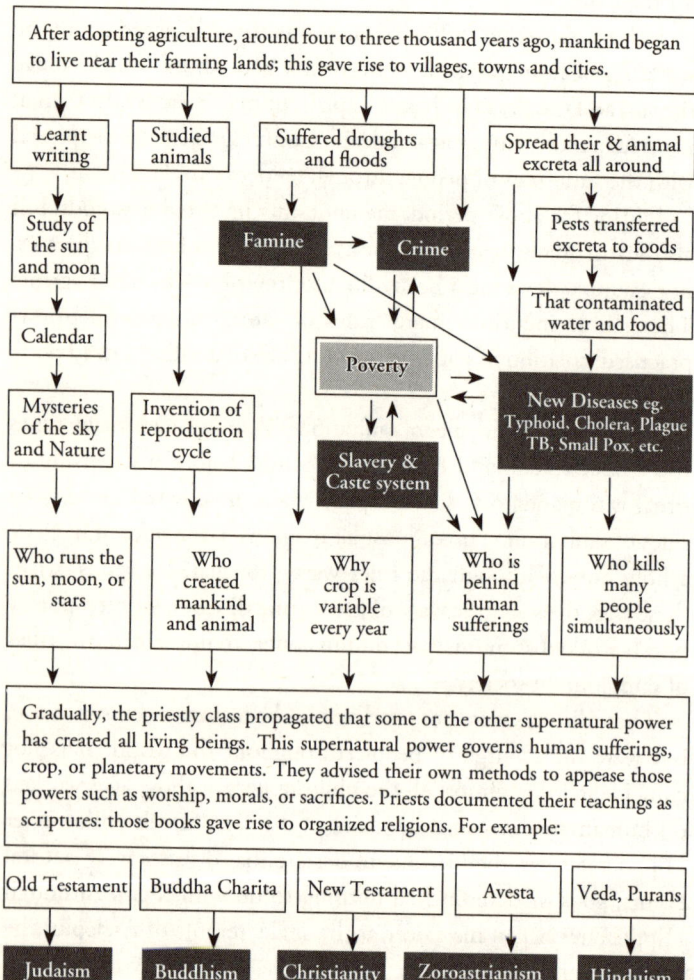

Illustration of Origin of Organized Religions

Unquestionably, he was the father of scientific medicine, being the first to enlighten the world with his rational approach to the cause and treatment of diseases. Hippocrates wrote that tuberculosis was the most prevalent chronic disease in his time.

After Hippocrates, another Greek philosopher Aristotle (384–322 BCE) continued his work. He was the son of a physician, and later became a tutor to Alexander the Great. He initiated the study of the structure and functioning of the human body. The last great figure in ancient scientific medicine, Claudius Galen, was born in 131 CE. He continued the work of Hippocrates and Aristotle and wrote many books. Galen described four classic symptoms of inflammation, i.e., redness, pain, fever and swelling. He studied the internal structures of humans by dissecting dead bodies.

Historians believe that the death of Galen was the beginning of the dark age of medicine. After his demise, the scientific approach to diseases was strangled for the next 1,500 years. During that long period, the popularity of theological doctrines created darkness among the masses.

Mankind always had an instinct to explore the mysteries around. During this period, even philosophers unwillingly closed their eyes before serious diseases. There must have been some radical change of thought that rendered men to behave like puppets. They tolerated many miseries, but made no serious effort to counter them. The cause of the darkness was as small as a seed but gave rise to a big tree later.

King Constantine adopted Christianity in the fourth century CE. After this, gradually, Christianity became a popular religion, and the Bible came to be considered the most authentic book and source of all information and wisdom. The end of the fifth century witnessed the downfall of the Greek and the Roman Empires. Disintegration of these empires resulted in anarchy. In the midst of chaos, Christianity emerged as the only cementing force.

Gradually, papacy established itself as a dominant world force through its missionaries and educational work. Papacy was declared independent of the state. The missionaries began to educate the masses. They guided the masses by the rules of God mentioned in the Bible. Monasticism became the preferred way of life.

Priests practised magic tricks for healing. They cared for mentally ill patients by praying and touching them. They prescribed potions in the waning phase of the moon. Although priests provided good care and nursing, no efforts were made to think about the cause of diseases.

Treatment of lepers mentioned in the Old Testament has been discussed earlier. The Bible of the Christians, the New Testament, narrates the miracles performed by Jesus. For example, it mentions: 'Jesus cured a man possessed with a devil. He cast out the devil within him and threw it onto a herd of swine. Soon, the animals became possessed and ran violently down a steep place into the sea.'

Another example: 'Jesus arrived at Peter's house, his mother-in-law was sick in bed with a high fever. Jesus touched her hand, the fever left her. Then she got up and prepared a meal for him. That evening many other demon-possessed people were brought to Jesus. He cast out the evil spirits with a simple command, and he healed all the sick. Jesus touched a leper and said, "Be healed," and the leprosy disappeared immediately. Jesus said to the leper, "Do not tell anyone about this. Go to the priest and let him examine you. Take along the mandatory offerings in the Law of Moses for healed lepers. The sacrifice would be a public testimony that you have been cleansed."' According to the law of Moses, sacrifice of three lambs was mandatory to clean a leper.

These magical remedies mentioned in the Bible were said to be revealed by God. Obviously, no one could dare to contradict the words of God. Every priest studied the Bible and knew that the devils caused diseases. After the study of the Bible, priests considered themselves as learned. In fact, they developed an illusion of knowledge. The greatest obstacle to discovery was not ignorance, but the illusion of knowledge.

During that time, rationalists were not allowed to contradict any rule of the Bible. Thus, the theory of the Bible arrested all the inventions of the medical field. Books written by Hippocrates and Galen were burnt. The darkness of the medical field created by the Bible continued for almost two millennia. Only recently, the light of modern science managed to vanquish it.

Not only Rome, imperialist ambitions of Christians gradually converted the major population of the globe. Thus, new converts also followed the rules of the Bible. In fact, the Bible and other ancient books obscured the path towards reason. Besides, the concept of disease-causing demons gave rise to further abuse of religions through witchcraft, sorcery or tantra.

At the end of the first millennium CE, the increasing population of the cities resulted in a further complex society. Inequality, exploitation and injustice plagued the masses. Ambition and jealousy facilitated rivalry and revenge. Hitherto, priests had been performing many magical tricks to cure patients by casting demons away. Gradually, some priests began to claim that they could control the demons. They used these demons to bless their clients with wine, women and wealth.

Furthermore, People began deploying these demons to take revenge. They tried to hurt their enemy with the help of demons. Logically, they were correct. The people already knew that demons of diseases were capable enough to hurt anybody. By now, society had made laws to punish any violence. Now, demons became very useful to seek revenge because they left no footprint of their crime.

This abuse of religion was a global phenomenon. To hurt the enemy through some magical rituals was the most consistent feature of all religions. The process had distinct names, such as witchcraft, sorcery, tantra, etc. Worldwide, people invented many magical rituals, potions, mimicries and amulets to harm their mighty enemies. These practices can be portrayed well by the description of witchcraft practised by Europeans, since they documented eyewitness accounts.

Witchcraft in Europe began around a thousand years ago or earlier. The people already believed that their illnesses were caused by demons. Now, they began to believe that the demons were sent by their enemies through witchcraft. The witches were those males or females who could control demons and hurt anyone. To hurt the enemy, witches caused illnesses, sterility, theft, etc.

For example, a father of four children believed a barren woman to be his enemy. Unfortunately, he suffered from tuberculosis. Soon, he blamed that woman for having caused his illness through some witchcraft. Or say, a young boy was attracted to a married woman. In this situation people believed that she applied some witchcraft on the boy in order to attract him. During that time, even if some potter found his clay pots broken, he blamed some witch. People believed that witches could transform themselves into animals or birds, make someone impotent, poison food and cause diseases.

Administrators declared that any effort of sorcery or witchcraft would be considered blasphemous and strictly punished. The more they castigated witchcraft, the more it flourished. In 1374 CE, Roman executives declared that magic was done with the help of some demon, and it must be considered an act against God. This way they themselves averred the existence of demons.

In 1484 CE, executives ordered to search and hunt down witches. Two officers were deputed who, after two years of research, wrote a book regarding identification of witches. This official book, *Malleus Maleficarum* or *The Hammer of Witches*, was first published in 1486 CE. The book details methods of identification and punishment of witches. It was a misogynist book as it blamed mainly females for witchcraft. The book was reprinted twenty-eight times till 1600 CE.

The Hammer of Witches mentions that witches were those females who consorted with some demon due to their insatiable sex desire. After the tryst, the female became possessed with the demon: she could use that demon as she desired. Sudden loss of reason or mental disorientation was the main symptom of demonic possession. Thus, all mentally ill females were considered witches. Other than mentally challenged females, middle-aged, lonely and infertile females were commonly accused of witchcraft. Other signs of witches were red spots on the skin and loss of sensation. These were supposed to be love marks made by the devil during their tryst.

Witch identification generally began with suspicion of a patient about his illness. Commonly, some chronic patient began suspecting some female witch behind his illness. He disclosed his doubt to his acquaintances. Gradually, it became a public rumour about that particular female. The victim made the first accusation. The complaint was lodged, and a judge heard the proceedings. It was believed that local judges, who were aware of the local beliefs, were more inclined to convict the accused. On the contrary, outsider judges were not prejudiced, so they usually acquitted the accused.

The trials were commonly a public affair. The officer used to interrogate the accused about her intercourse or interaction with the devil. On her denial, they simply tortured the woman considered to be a witch. The woman shouted, but the more she shouted, the more flogging she received. She was sure that she slept alone, but the officer was adamant that she was with some devil the night before. She knew that she would be tortured until she confessed to the desired act: it was wiser to lie. Her psychosis was less than the psychosis of the executive beating her. Her confession about meeting with the demon brought a victorious smile to the officer. Those confessions confirmed the existence of witchcraft in the eyes of the masses. After the confession, the judge sentenced her to death and executioners burnt her alive. According to one estimate, around fifty thousand people, mostly females, were burnt alive in several European countries during the period 1450–1750.

All religions of the world practised witchcraft in the way more or less as described above. In the last millennium, thousands of innocent people were accused and punished for practising witchcraft as there was no evidence either to prove or disprove it.

Scientific medicine could not progress until the nineteenth century. Promoters of all religions dissuaded people from writing scientific books. Any concept contrary to those mentioned in the old scriptures was considered blasphemous. Not only witches, priests also convicted and punished many scientists. Study of anatomy of the dead was considered heresy in many places. Religions regularly strangulated the voice of scientists until the nineteenth century. During the last two thousand years, religious scriptures deferred scientific progress of mankind. For example, smallpox was considered a disease sent by an angry god. In the nineteenth century, religious authorities prohibited vaccination for smallpox because it was supposed to intervene with the divine affair.

The invention of the microscope at the end of the sixteenth century laid the foundation of modern medicine in Holland. Medical science began to use this device in the middle of the seventeenth century. The Royal Society of London was given a royal charter in 1662 CE, which began the first scientific study of diseases. Gradually, in the next three centuries, mankind came out of the previous ignorant state. In this period, scientists tried their best to understand the causes of epidemic diseases.

Louis Pasteur, in 1858 CE, discovered that tiny organisms not seen by naked eyes were causing the communicable diseases. After this discovery, priests who continued to believe the god-and-demon theory were slowly sidelined.

Today, microbiologists know that micro-organisms caused all the epidemic diseases of the early farmers. Every such organism had its own optimum temperature and humidity to survive and divide. Given the opportunity, one such micro-organism could reproduce, giving birth to billions of similar creatures within a day. That was the reason a particular illness emerged in a particular season.

These micro-organisms show two kinds of behaviour: commensal and pathogenic. Commensals are micro-organisms who live comfortably on animals without causing any disease. Pathogens are microbes which invade animals by different routes and multiply to cause diseases. Commensal bacteria living comfortably on one animal species are usually pathogens for other species.

Before adopting agriculture, men had not domesticated animals, so they were not exposed to the commensals of animals. Domestication necessitated living together with animals. Many commensals living on the pets behaved pathogenically on men and caused diseases. According to an American scholar William McNeill, humans shared some sixty-five diseases with dogs, fifty with cattle, forty-six with sheep, forty-two with pigs, thirty-five with horses and twenty-six with poultry. The data indicate that infections to humans were mainly gifted by domestic animals.

There is enough evidence to prove that men became the most diseased animal on the earth after adoption of agriculture. The fact that nomadic people were healthier is further attested by the discovery of many healthy aborigines. For example, Alfred Crosby has mentioned that at least twenty-five infectious diseases were unknown to the Native Americans. Furthermore, British colonization of Australia began in Sydney in 1788. The most immediate consequence of British settlement, within weeks, was a wave of epidemic disease.

Besides, nomads frequently changed their settlements that protected them from contagious diseases. They were drinking pure water, better than the best mineral water brands we have today. The stay of farmers was permanent, long enough to pollute the drinking water sources. Leftovers of farmers served as rich media for bacteria to thrive. Farmers also received commensals of rodents and cats living with them.

Men rarely received a disease from wild animals in the forest. This fact can be understood by the example of Human Immunodeficiency Virus that causes AIDS. This virus came from a wild African chimpanzee, *Pan troglodytes*. After finding a way to reach the human blood, it changed its structure and began to behave as a pathogen. It was detected in 1981, and mankind might have first contracted the disease only a few decades earlier. Had the chimp been domesticated, men would have had AIDS far earlier, and that could have finished the human race. The curious question is how the virus reached the bloodstream of the first infected patient? Possibly, some wild chimp bit a homosexual man, later he spread it in his community.

Robert Koch (1830–1910 CE) identified the causative organism of cholera that caused diarrhoea discussed earlier. The episode was an outcome of consuming contaminated water from a common source. Water was contaminated by the bacteria present in the faeces of the town dwellers. Similarly, Robert Koch identified the causative organism of tuberculosis. Microbiologists believe that its bacteria lived on cattle. After domestication, man began drinking cattle milk without boiling, and the bacteria reached the human intestine.

The dreaded disease of plague was also caused by bacteria called *Yersinia pestis*, which lived on rats. Bacteria usually caused no disease to rats. Bodies of rats usually had another parasite called fleas which sucked their blood. Whenever a rat died, parasite fleas left the body of the rat like passengers of a sinking ship. If one of these hungry fleas bit a man, it injected the bacteria of the rat into his bloodstream. Soon, the man suffered from plague. Rats began to live within human settlements to feast on stored foodgrains of farmers. Today, doctors can prevent or kill the age-old demon of plague just by a course of antibiotic tetracycline, costing fifty rupees.

In the last two millennia, deadly epidemics of plague have killed billions. Usually, the people faced flood or drought every second or third year, which was commonly followed by an epidemic. Man, the wisest animal on earth, said to be the best creation of God, spent his days in fear of diseases during that long period. Fortunately, they had already enforced a taboo on incest, which increased their immunity and thus chances of survival. Outbreeding increased the adaptability and resistance power of men and thus saved them from extinction.

The cause of increased incidences of witches all over Europe was a matter of debate in modern times. Various theological, political and medical reasons were considered. In 1976, Linda Caporael explained the strange behaviour of the supposed witches. She proposed a scientific reason which resolved all the confusion.

Ergot is a parasitic fungus which grows on food in a warm and humid season. The fungus contains a drug that can cause tingling, vertigo, headache, hallucination, mania and depression. These are the symptoms which common witches used to have. It is likely that the victims were consuming the fungus accidentally grown over their food. There are enough reasons to believe that ergot poisoning was the cause of strange behaviour of convicted witches. Not only ergot, hysteria is a common disorder in young ladies. Its usual symptoms are also similar to the behaviour of the supposed witches.

Other historians believe that some of the convicted witches performed actual murders. In a famous case in 1324 CE in Ireland, Lady Alice Kyteller was charged with performing magical rites, having sexual intercourse with demons, attempting to divine the future and poisoning her first three husbands.

In fact, in those days, there were no books or chemical suppliers that could guide someone about poisons. Only rare people knew about poisons. During that time, knowledge of poison could make anyone a magical person. Since medical people could not detect the trace of poison in a dead body, many poisoned victims were supposed to be killed by witchcraft.

Human sufferings gifted by civilization continued until recently. Sir Alexander Fleming discovered the first antibiotic penicillin in 1940. It is a magic drug for almost all bacterial infections including syphilis. Soon, streptomycin joined the war against diseases. It is a wonder drug for the age-old demon of tuberculosis.

In the last fifty years, humanity has conquered almost every disease. It is a result of the marathon researches undertaken over the last three hundred years. Mankind today practises evidence-based medicine. Medical scientists know the cause of almost every ailment. Almost all infections except the viral ones are curable now: vaccination is there for prevention of viral diseases.

After eradicating smallpox, plague and polio, humanity has killed three demons that were beyond the control of all gods for centuries. Rotarians deserve special appreciation for their sincere and honest efforts to vaccinate infants all over the globe. Men could find cures for these diseases only after they discarded the knowledge of ancient books.

Psychosis is still the dark field of medicine. Even today, many priests are treating psychotics through casting demons away. They still believe that cause of psychosis is possession by demons. Commonly, Hindu and Muslim psychotic patients can be seen at holy places for treatment. Hundreds of temples and mosques had a system to treat psychotic patients.

For treatment, the patient is taken to those holy places and asked to worship. Priests prescribe some potion or amulet to the patients. The holy places of Hindus are usually temples of one or the other god. Muslim holy places are commonly the graves of some famous saints.

These religious places are also used frequently for witchcraft-like activities. Yes, even today, witchcraft is widely practised. Many sorcerers run their shops, solve every problem under the sun and people believe them too.

Today, old diseases are no more nightmares for people, but many new diseases have emerged in the last fifty years. In fact, the lifestyle of modern men is characterized by the explosion of food availability and reduction of physical labour. Ambition, possessiveness, arrogance, greed and jealousy characterize much of human behaviour. The preference for individualism over community has rendered the common man lonely and depressed.

This new lifestyle of men has exposed them to new diseases like obesity, diabetes, hypertension, heart disease, mental illness, etc. Today, doctors have many drugs to control these illnesses but no drug to prevent them. These new diseases can be prevented by yoga or physical exercise.

Only twenty-five years ago, people recognized the ancient art of yoga for health benefits. The last ten years have seen a tremendous rise in people's faith in yoga round the globe. Yoga can protect anyone from new diseases even without changing one's lifestyle. Meditation is capable of preventing and treating self-inflicted mental illnesses. Today neither prayers nor sacrifices are required for the prevention of diseases. Meditation and yoga are destined to be the ultimate religion in years to come.

After the study of the previous chapters, it is obvious that ancient people built many myths to wrestle with their problems. In fact, with the help of language and imagination, people began to fathom nature around them. Whatever they could not understand, they built myths to explain. Not only myths, imagination gave rise to many scientific theories too.

For example, Sir Isaac Newton saw an apple falling on the ground. He picked it up and dropped it again. He wondered why the apple returned to the ground every time. This had been happening since the world began, but Newton was the first to question and seek an explanation for it. No one before him had thought in the way he had. He imagined an unseen force pulling the apple towards the earth.

The first thought of Newton was an exercise in imagination, but later he proved it to establish a scientific law. Thus, every generation taught various concepts to the next. Later, some of these concepts were proven to be myths, but the rest were scientific. Men invented religion, mythology, art, literature and even science by their unique power of imagination.

Spoken languages enabled men to carry forward scientific inventions. This brought about a progression and thus ensured a better living with each passing generation. Today, the results are already there for everyone to see. Stone tools to atom bombs, bark canoes to huge ships, paper planes to spacecrafts – all these were developed by the endeavours of many generations. It has been a progressive improvement which took thousands of generations to attain. Imagination and language made it possible to invent, propagate and accumulate all the religions and science that mankind has today.

From the first chapter till now, the religious activities of mankind have been discussed in general. After writing was invented, religious activities, teachings and myths were documented as the holy books. Subsequent generations of priests preserved these sacred books. These books gave rise to modern religions. The next chapters will discuss the histories of the three major religions individually.

7

Hinduism

Hinduism is the oldest surviving religion of the world. Ancient inhabitants of Indian subcontinent discovered this religion much earlier than the word 'Hindu' came into practice. Ancient Hindu scriptures such as the Vedas, Ramayana, Mahabharata, Puranas or any other ancient Hindu book do not mention the word Hindu. In fact, the word Hindu was used only after the eighth century CE. It was the name given to the people living on the bank of the river Indus. Thus, the Indians living in the earlier period cannot be called Hindus. To avoid confusion, the word Hindu is being used here for the inhabitants of the Indian subcontinent of any age.

Around five thousand years ago, and even earlier, Hindus began developing many beliefs and practices to wrestle with the challenges they faced. With time, a lot of these became obsolete, several were tailored to changing needs, various new ideas were invented to fight new problems and many remained vestigial. Amalgamation of these beliefs and practices of different times gave rise to modern Hinduism.

Abundant in diverse customs, Hinduism is supplemented by many holy books. The entire lifetime of a scholar is not enough to read all of them. During different time periods of Hinduism, people practised various styles of worship and sacrifices. For example, they practised the nature worship of tribesmen, the sacrifices analogous to Jews, the moral code like Christians and monotheism similar to Muslims. Just by studying the history of Hinduism, one can learn all the evolutionary stages of the concept of god in the world.

Hinduism has one basic difference from other organized religions of the world. Prophets of most religions proclaimed that their god revealed the holy book of the religion they founded. On the contrary, no Hindu saint, not even the Buddha, ever claimed that he met any god personally. Hindu saints wrote many books about gods but did not claim that some god revealed the holy text to them. Therefore, no Hindu religious book is widely accepted to be revealed by any god himself.

This deficiency, despite its honesty, has made Hinduism the most malleable religion of the world. Some scholars opine that it does not qualify as religion. Hinduism is better defined as a way of leading a happy life through morals, worship and rituals.

The earliest evidence of the religion practised by the people of Indian subcontinent was excavated from the Indus Valley. In the 1920s, archaeologists discovered a whole civilization buried along the plains of the Indus. Many small villages and two big cities were excavated in this territory stretching over present-day Pakistan and India.

The Indus Valley civilization flourished between 3500 to 1500 BCE. This was the time when Egyptians built pyramids for the luxuries of the dead bodies of their kings, and Mesopotamians made ziggurats for their sun worship.

The people of the Indus Valley were early farmers. The earliest writings of the world, written about 5,500 years ago, have been excavated here. Since these inscriptions have not yet been deciphered, the religious practices of the people are not understood well. Only a few shreds of their worship are available that can provide just a glimpse of their faiths.

For example, archaeologists found phallic symbols and female statues in the Indus Valley. These are similar to the fertility symbols made by early farmers round the globe. Apart from these, many seals were excavated here showing pictures of trees and animals. One of the seals depicts the image of a seated male. Historians associate this sculpture with god Shiva.

In the excavations of a city only a few such sculptures were found. This indicates that every family did not keep them in their house. At the same time, these are not big enough to be used for worship in a community place. These might be simply works of art rather than depiction of deities.

In the Valley, many graves were excavated showing simple burial rituals. The corpses were buried along with food, tools and ornaments. This indicates that the people believed that there remained some life after death. In the Indus Valley, there was no architecture that could be recognized as a temple – the public place of worship. Surprisingly, a civilization that flourished for two millennia, over a huge geographical area, had no public place of worship. People built thousands of brick houses but not a single temple. It is likely that they worshiped the sun and the sky that required no temple or idol. This thought is further supported by the fact that contemporary Vedic people also built no temple for almost three millennia and worshipped the sun and the sky.

Other than the Indus Valley civilization, the oldest evidence of Hindu religion is found in northern India. Around five thousand years ago, and even earlier, the people of northern India began practising the Vedic religion. There are diverse opinions about when the Vedic teachings began.

Many historians believe that the Vedic hymns were composed around five thousand years ago. Scholars such as Bal Gangadhar

Tilak believed that Vedic priests initiated the composition of hymns far earlier. Many other historians believe that the Vedic religion began prior to the Indus Valley civilization. They claim that many Vedic traditions are older than those of the Indus Valley.

Similar to all other civilizations, priests of the Vedic times evolved and taught this religion. These priests were called Arya, which means noble. These priests were the cornerstones of the society and earned their livelihood through intellectual work. They taught people to use fire to protect them from wild animals and ghosts. They invented magical and herbal remedies to treat patients. They developed various rituals and sacrifices to be performed at the time of birth, marriage, harvest, death and natural calamities.

They composed many Vedic hymns to please the nature gods and taught these to the masses. Thus, the Vedic priests worked as priests, doctors and teachers of society. The Vedic priests were the Indian counterparts of the priests who emerged with the rise of agriculture all over the world.

Vedic hymns were mainly short flattering poems addressed to nature gods. Some hymns narrated the methods of worship and rituals. These hymns were taught in boarding schools called Gurukuls. Priests dictated the hymns and students repeated them verbally to memorize them. After schooling, students chanted these hymns for the rest of their lives. Thus, the hymns were passed on from one generation to another orally, without being written.

Later, these priests invented writing and wrote down these hymns. Most ancient Vedic hymns were compiled in the Rig Veda – the oldest surviving literature of the world. Again, there is a vast variation in opinions about the date of the Rig Veda's transcription. Most historians believe that the priests began writing the Rig Veda around 3,400 years ago or even earlier.

Unlike contemporary literature of the globe, the Vedas do not narrate the history of their time. The Vedas precisely depict the religious beliefs of the contemporary people. The Rig Veda has many hymns dedicated to each of the Vedic gods. Many hymns convey similar meaning, and they read: 'Oh god you are great; you gave us life; you protect us; kindly have mercy on us; kindly bless us.' This indicates that hundreds of poets must have contributed to the Rig Veda. It is likely, that priests of different places composed their own hymns to glorify each of their gods, and later all of them were compiled into one book.

Most historians believe that the Vedic people were farmers. They worshipped the sun, the sky and fire. They practised animal sacrifice regularly to appease their gods. The most important Vedic god was the sun. The hymns of the Rig Veda portray the sun as the only sustainer of all the life on the earth.

Vedic priests believed the sun to be the source of unlimited power and radiance. It was responsible for the change of seasons and protected people from cold. Sunlight was known to cure diseases and keep everyone healthy. Priests composed Gayatri mantra to worship the rising sun. Even today, many Hindus start their day with the chanting of the Gayatri mantra. Meaning of a few of the hymns dedicated to the sun is as follows:

> Always indulging in auspicious deeds,
> Sun raises his arms to give us alms.
> He raises his arms to keep the world in balance.
> May we constantly get gifts from him.
> He grants stability to all beings.
> He created them.
> Let all humans beg for friendship of the sun.
> O sun god! Please fulfil our desire.
> Inspire all the gods to keep our enemies away.
> O sun god! provide us happiness.
> We are singing hymns to him to get
> cereals, money and happiness.

Another important Vedic god was the sky god. He had many names according to his different attributes, such as Marut, Varuna, Rudra or Indra. The sky god was responsible for the wind, the storms and the rain. He regulated the weather and his weapon, the lightning, brought rain. The Vedic people believed that the sky god blessed them with good harvest, health and fertility. At the same time his anger destroyed the same. For example the meaning of one hymn for the sky god is as follows:

> O Rudra, slay us not, nor desert us.
> When you are angry, do not ruin us.
> You are lord of sacrifices, hymns and medicines,
> We pray for joy, health and strength.
> You shine like the sun, as bright as gold.
> You are the good, the best, among the gods.
> May you grant health to us and our cattle.

Another most worshipped Vedic god was Agni, the fire god, who protected people from the cold, wild animals and ghosts. A large number of hymns of the Rig Veda are dedicated to Agni. Meaning of a few hymns is as follows:

> Like the sun, Agni enlightens all things.
> Even though the sun is the king of gods,
> Agni nourishes us like cow's milk.
> Agni! Even demons cannot disturb your yajna.
> Demons are scared off by you with the help of wind.
> Agni shakes the clouds to shed rains.
> O Agni, shine brilliantly to provide wealth.
> Be pleased with our hymns and protect us.
> Please destroy our enemies near or far away.

The Rig Veda consists of around one thousand more or less similar hymns about all the three gods. A few centuries after the Rig

Veda, three more Vedas were composed. The Sama Veda is merely a repetition of the hymns in the Rig Veda. Yajur Veda is a manual that lists the techniques of sacrifices, in prose. The Atharva Veda is a compilation of herbal and magical remedies of diseases.

Not only did priests initiate the chanting of rhymes, they also developed soma, rituals and animal sacrifices to appease the nature gods. Soma was a hallucinogenic drink. Its importance can be assessed by the fact that a major section of the Rig Veda is dedicated to describe the divine experiences after the intake of this drink.

Many modern Hindus believe that soma was some alcoholic drink. In fact, it was prepared by crushing the leaves of a plant called hemp (bhang). After drinking it, the person experienced euphoria or ecstasy. Soma was consumed during each ritual. One hymn mentions the experience of Indra after drinking soma. This may be the experience of the poet who wrote it. Its meaning is as follows:

> The heavens above do not equal one half of me.
> Have I been drinking soma?
> I have passed beyond the sky and the earth.
> Have I been...
> I will pick up the earth and put it here or put it there.
> Have I been...

The most important Vedic ritual was the yajna which is widely practised even today. Yajna is a Sanskrit word which means sacrifice. Yajna was a sacrificial burning of different edibles dedicated to the fire god. After studying the hymns dedicated to fire, it becomes obvious that the practice of yajna initiated as a worship of simple fireplaces. It must have begun well before the Vedic hymns were made.

In fact, the earliest yajna was called Aupasana. This Yajna was performed twice a day into each household fireplace that smouldered round the clock in each home. This yajna was a simple worship of fire. People offered some food into their domestic fireplace every day. Thus, yajna initiated as the worship of hearths or fireplaces.

During the earlier Vedic time weather was far colder than it is today and so fireplaces were mandatory to survive. Besides, fireplaces gave them light and protection from wild animals after dusk. Igniting fire was a difficult job; so smouldering fireplaces were maintained to ignite a new fire every time.

The Vedic people had only bamboos to protect them. They were easy prey to wild animals during the night. The smoke of the fireplaces protected them from wild animals throughout the night. Even today, many Hindus do not extinguish the fire after the yajna. Similar to the ancient fireplaces, after the end of a yajna, they leave charred wood smoking overnight.

All over the globe, many contemporary people maintained fireplaces round the clock and worshipped them. Utility of fire and the difficulty of igniting it bestowed a divine status on the fireplaces among Vedic people too. In the evening, they sat around the fireplace and drank the intoxicating drink soma. They observed the flaring up of the flames after eatable items were thrown into the fire. They must have perceived this flaring up as cheerfulness of fire. They conceived that giving their own food was like a sacrifice to the fire god, which appeased him.

As discussed earlier, Vedic priests composed many hymns to worship all the nature gods. After composing hymns, they ignited fireplaces after chanting the hymns dedicated to the fire god, Agni. A typical hymn to ignite a fireplace runs like this:

> O Agni! Please accept our hymns!
> You are like a brother and friend to all.
> You deserve appreciation from all.
> O Agni! Let this yajna be completed for our sake,
> dedicated to the sun, Rudra, and other gods.

> Please depart to the venue of the yajna,
> to complete the ceremony.

Gradually, priests initiated the chanting of different hymns before the sacrifice of food into the fireplace. After hearing each hymn, people sitting around threw food into the fireplace. With time, priests began the sacrifice of food in the name of other gods too.

Gradually, generations of Vedic priests designated yajna as a ritual to propitiate all the gods. In the late Vedic period, Yajna was performed routinely on all occasions such as for purifying a house, treating patients, seeking rain, etc. Furthermore, priests made the provision of donation for themselves. After completion of each yajna, they anticipated donation of clothes, cereals or cows.

Historian AL Basham has written that during the earlier Vedic period, yajna was a domestic affair. After a long duration of a millennium, in the later Vedic period, it gradually attained the grandeur of a spectacular public function. Fireplaces were modified to large altars. Thus, Vedic priests gradually modified the domestic fireplace to yajna as a ritual to propitiate all the gods. In his famous book, *The Wonder That Was India*, AL Basham has portrayed an eyewitness account of yajna as follows:

> Nevertheless, the ceremony must have had its element of awe and wonder. The worshippers, inebriated with soma, saw wondrous vision of gods; they experienced strange sensations of power; they could reach up and touch the heavens; they became immortal; they were gods themselves. The priests, who alone knew the rituals and formulae whereby the gods were brought to the sacrifice, were masters of a great mystery.

From the late Vedic period till date, Hindus have been performing yajna consistently at the time of birth, marriage and death. Besides, Hindus consider yajna mandatory before beginning any new venture like a business or entering a new house. A typical Hindu marriage ceremony essentially consists of a yajna performed by the couple. At the end of the yajna, the couple circumambulates the altar so as to be witnessed as a couple by the fire god.

Nowadays, yajna is performed on a raised square platform called bedi, the altar. This is made of mud and bricks. Chunks of wood are arranged in a specific fashion after the alter is made. The performing priest prepares a mixture of inflammable food materials such as sesame seeds, rice, barley, sugar and animal milk fat; this mixture is called samagri.

Worshippers sit around the altar and do a ritual worship of the sun, the moon, Indra and all the planets. The priest ignites the fire while chanting the hymns of the fire god. After the appearance of flames, the priest chants other holy hymns of the Rig Veda and ends each time with the word 'swaha'. Each worshipper repeats the word and then offers a pinch of the herbal mixture (samagri) into the fire. The food materials burnt in the fire are supposed to ultimately reach the divine entity. At the end of each yajna, the performing priest collects donations on behalf of all the gods.

Let's consider why Hindus have been burning food materials to perform yajna for many millennia. Firstly, ancient priests propagated that these foods satiated the sun, the sky and the fire god. Obviously, these gods must be hungry and the priests burnt food to satiate their hunger. Not only Hindus, many ancient people believed the same. Aztecs sacrificed humans and burnt their hearts to satiate their god.

Most Vedic priests were worked as teachers and doctors besides being priests. They spent most of their time serving the community. It has already been discussed that people did not pay any service charges to priests. Their services were perceived as charity. Vedic priests intelligently planned the ritual of yajna in such a way that the masses had to pay them regularly. Today, there is no logical reason behind such burning of food, which only contributes to pollution. It would be far better to donate food to the poor.

Vedic people did not know any modern Hindu gods such as Ram, Krishna or Durga. In fact, Vedic people had not yet personified their gods. The idolatry – the essence of today's Hinduism – was largely unknown. Although the Vedic people were apparently polytheist, they began to visualize monotheism, like the rest of the contemporary world. For example, a hymn of the Rig Veda narrates: 'God is one, but people call Him by different names.' Thus, the Vedic people initiated a belief that there must be one ultimate cause that accounts for all the mysteries of nature, but they were not sure of its exact form.

Today, many modern Hindu religious teachers claim that they have studied the Vedas. They propagate that the Vedas are collections of great knowledge. Common Hindus also believe the same. However, this is debatable. The hymns from the Rig Veda quoted earlier give an indication of the knowledge compiled in the Vedas which chiefly contain poems glorifying nature gods. At least in the context of today, the value of information contained in the Vedas is highly debatable.

The major importance of the Vedas lies in their antiquity. These are the oldest surviving writings in the world. At the same time, they are invaluable to understand the thoughts and challenges faced by the Vedic people living in those times.

It is obvious that those people were wise enough to understand that their life was dependent upon the sun, the sky and fire. All these were beyond their control. Therefore, priests composed flattering rhymes to please these forces of nature. Common men chanted these hymns regularly to be blessed by them.

The description of the Vedic religion is incomplete without the mention of asceticism – the soul of Hindu religion. Vedic priests propagated two methods to achieve divine magical powers: yajna and asceticism. Yajna was performed by the tribal chiefs and merchants; priests and the poor preferred asceticism.

Asceticism is called 'tapasya' in Sanskrit. It was a type of devotional worship that was performed through self-torture. Priests believed that gods could be appeased through devoting some of their worldly comforts. For example, tapasya was commonly performed in the depths of forests, where people tortured themselves through abstinence, hunger, thirst, living austerely, facing adverse weather or endangering themselves to the attacks of wild animals.

For tapasya, many people invented various techniques. For example, they hung themselves on the stout branches of trees for hours, head downward. Some others held their one hand motionless towards the sky until that atrophied. Many ascetics searched some inaccessible spot in the forests or mountains; there they performed tapasya unflaggingly for months and years.

After such a spell of tapasya or self-torture, they believed that they were blessed with divine powers. They were respected by the masses as well after performing such tapasya. Common men also had the conviction that through tapasya a person could attain divine powers. Many saints, after prolonged asceticism, were worshipped as gods.

Indian masses continued Vedic worship and animal sacrifices till the end of the Vedic period – 2,500 years ago. Around 2,500 years ago, a great man took birth in India; his teachings are followed by almost half the world's population. During that time, Sakya was a small tribe in the Himalayan foothills. The wife of the king of the Sakya clan gave birth to a prince, Siddhartha. The prince spent his childhood in his palace with all possible worldly comforts. His father observed that the child was different from his peers: he was thoughtful and non-violent. Siddhartha was married to a princess at the age of nineteen. After ten years of marriage, his wife gave birth to a son, Rahul. After some time, Siddhartha realized that human life was full of sufferings such as diseases, debilities and death.

After this knowledge, Siddhartha gave up his worldly comforts to find a remedy for the miseries of the masses. He left his family and kingdom and lived as an ascetic in a dense forest. There he meditated for six years. He tortured his body by all means. At last, he meditated day and night under a banyan tree without eating anything. On the fortieth day, Siddhartha achieved his famous enlightenment.

Siddhartha was now called the Buddha that means the Enlightened One. The enlightenment of the Buddha was not a meeting with some god or any angel in person. Neither had he heard some god's voice from the sky. It was an understanding of the causes and remedies for all human miseries under the sun. The Buddha advocated four Noble Truths that described the causes and remedies of human miseries. During one sermon delivered at Varanasi, the Buddha narrated his teachings as follows:

> *This is the Noble Truth of Life*: Birth is sorrow, age is sorrow, death is sorrow, disease is sorrow, company of an idiot is sorrow, desertion of a dear one is sorrow and every unfulfilled wish is sorrow.
>
> *This is the Noble Truth of Arising of Sorrows*: These arise from the thirst for pleasure, the thirst for love, the thirst for sensual pleasure, the thirst for long life, the thirst for power. Thus all human thirsts lead to sorrow and ultimately rebirth.
>
> *This is the Noble Truth to Prevent Sorrows*: The complete renunciation of thirsts so that there is no passion, no desire and no lust. Annihilate the worldly desires, leave all these and allow them no space in life.
>
> *This is the Noble Truth to Stop Sorrows*: It is the Noble Eightfold Path: Right Views, Right Resolve, Right Speech, Right Conduct, Right Livelihood, Right Effort, Right Recollection and Right Meditation.

Thus, the Buddha discovered that human life was full of sufferings. Birth of every person was a spell of punishment. Humans suffered this punishment on account of their sins committed in their previous births. Thus, each human birth and death was like being punished again and again. The Buddha proclaimed that human life could be improved by good deeds. The Buddha did not suggest any devotion, prayer or ritual dedicated to some god or himself. He advocated that the most sacred conduct of man was 'ahimsa' – non-violent personal behaviour. His non-violence was not limited to physical injury only, but included mental harassment as well.

The Buddha advocated that the ultimate goal of each individual was to attain freedom from the cycle of births and deaths on the earth. He called it nirvana, the salvation. The Buddha preached that anyone could achieve nirvana after following the noble Eightfold Path throughout his life. To attain nirvana the Buddha also advised asceticism – to suppress worldly desires.

The Buddha popularized the practice of asceticism to the masses. He advised asceticism to achieve nirvana after death. Contrary to Vedic asceticism, it was not to achieve magical powers. Usually, Buddhists practised prolonged celibacy or fasting. All these practices were another kind of sacrifice. The essence of these practices still survives among modern Hindus.

The Buddha visited and preached at many places in India. Soon, people accepted his logical teachings. After his death, many of his followers taught and wrote down his teachings. Around two hundred years later, King Ashok accepted Buddhism. Ashok ruled over the large empire that his grandfather Chandragupta Maurya had created.

Ashok tried his best to spread the teachings of the Buddha through many stone inscriptions. These read: 'Do not do rituals for diseases, be gentle to even slaves, respect elders, treat all animals with love, give donations to monks and respect other religions.'

Ashok ordered the installation of many of these stone inscriptions all over India and even abroad.

Surprisingly, Ashok did not build any temple of the Buddha. In fact, the Buddha never asked people to worship him. The oldest idol of the Buddha was excavated in Mathura. It was made around five hundred years after his death. That was the time when people began worshiping the Buddha as god. By then, Buddhism had become the preferred religion of the masses of India.

The Buddha shaped an ideology that attracted almost half the population of the globe, in a period of one millennium. History has witnessed many followers of other organized religions who aggressively converted other people to their own faith by force or inducements.

Buddhism is the only religion that flourished mainly because of its excellent doctrine rather than fear or greed. The Buddha is the only religious teacher who preached the supremacy of deeds over worship. The Buddha is the greatest man to have been born in India, considering the magnitude of his influence on the world.

After the Buddha, the masses gradually developed an aversion towards Vedic sacrifices. Now, Hindus preferred non-violence and asceticism to Vedic rituals. At the same time, contemporary Vedic priests tried to preserve the ancient faith. For them, it was mandatory since the rituals were their only source of income.

Wise Vedic priests began to swim with the tide. They changed the concept of animal sacrifice and adopted non-violence. Vedic priests began to preach much of what the Buddha had taught but they also continued to worship the Vedic gods too. Thus, the masses performed yajna, gave donations, but refrained from animal sacrifice.

A few historians believe that the teachings of Jesus had been somewhat influenced by the Buddha. Jesus advised a similar philosophy of non-violence five hundred years later and tried to modify Judaism in the same way the Buddha modified the Vedic religion.

The Buddha propagated a well-crafted ideology in his lifetime. He was against Vedic rituals, the bread and butter of the priests. The Buddha's teachings would have rendered the priests unemployed.

Jesus could teach for a few years only. The Buddha taught for a long period of forty years. The Buddha became far more popular in his lifetime than Jesus Christ. He posed wider contradictions to the existing priests. However, Vedic priests did not try to imprison or humiliate him. It is worth considering that if the Buddha had been put to death by the entrenched priesthood of the time, Buddhism might have become the religion with the maximum following in the world.

After the death of the Buddha, the Vedic priests further modified their teachings. Between the third century BCE and the seventh century CE, a new Hindu religion emerged as an amalgamation of many religious concepts. The period witnessed personification of all the Vedic gods. The priests gave human shapes and attributes to the sun, the sky, and the fire gods. Idolatry – the essence of present-day Hinduism – was invented during this period.

Hindus began a new kind of relationship with their gods without taking the help of a priest. Hindus invented the worship of stone images to communicate with their gods directly. Now, the physical objects replaced the former abstract deities. These images were either natural or carved from stones in the shape of the sun, a human being or one of the human organs.

The stone images were fixed at the centre of square buildings called temples. These idols made it possible for Hindus to communicate with gods. Now people could show their devotion and reverence to god by touching the feet of the idol. They could express their love and affection for their gods by offering sweets.

Around 2,200 years ago, Hindus began the worship of the sun through a round and disc-shaped stone sculpture. They might have made icons of the sun earlier, but it is possible that they did not survive. A few coins belonging to this period exhibit a carved idol of the sun.

Gradually, the solar discs also displayed eyes, nose and lips. The ancient scripture of the Puranas mentions an antique temple of the sun in the Magadha region. Numerous ancient images of the sun have been found in the Gaya region of Bihar, and they are still worshipped on Sundays. The remains of an ancient sun temple of the first century CE were found at Martanda near Srinagar in Kashmir.

During the same period, Hindus began the worship of the sky god through Lingam – phallus-shaped stones. Historians believe that the Vedic period was followed by a sporadic development in the worship of the Lingam, around twenty-four centuries ago. However, Lingam worship might have begun much earlier, since the Indus Valley people also made phallic symbols.

The Lingam was either a carved or a natural phallus-shaped stone that was kept vertically for worship. Later, priests also made a horizontal platform to represent its female counterpart. Hindus worship only the upper round part of the stone Lingam, called Poojabhag, which means the portion of worship. It is also called Rudrabhag, which means the portion of Rudra – the sky god. Many historians advocate that the Lingam worshipped by Hindus was not a depiction of phallus. In fact, Lingam is the Sanskrit word for phallus, and there is enough evidence to attest its phallic origin. For example, the oldest surviving Lingam is the Gudimallam Linga situated in Andhra Pradesh, which was carved around 2,200 years ago. It is not only a round stone kept vertically but depicts the exact anatomy of the human phallus. Furthermore, a standing male figure is carved along its length.

Ancient Hindu scriptures also mention that Lingam was a depiction of phallus. For example, the epic Mahabharata has described the Lingam as the organ of reproduction of the supreme god. Besides, phallus worship was popular at many places of the globe during that period.

There is enough evidence to attest that the Lingam – the stone phallus – was a symbol to represent Rudra or Indra, the sky god. Why did wise priests deem the stone phallus to represent Indra? Why did not they depict Indra as a man similar to the sun?

Historians are usually silent about the reasons behind phallus worship. On the basis of ancient literature and other evidence, we may draw a logical conclusion. It is likely that after stone idols of the sun, contemporary priests must have tried to make an idol of another Vedic god Indra, the sky god as well.

The expressions of the sky god were wind, cloud, thunder, lightning or rain. It was difficult to carve the stone image of any of these. Besides, priests had a conviction that Indra, the sky god, is a single invisible power that delivers wind, cloud, thunder, lightning and rain. For example, the Rig Veda mentions:

> Let me describe the valiant deeds of Indra:
> First he is the master of the thunder,
> He slays the dragon of lightning
> And lets loose the rain.
> He pierces the bellies of mountains.

On one hand, Indra was invisible, and on the other, his manifestations (clouds, wind, rain, etc.) were difficult to depict. In this situation, contemporary Hindu priests must have stretched their imaginations to search for some symbol to represent the invisible sky god Indra. A symbol is usually an object that represents something else and shares some resemblance in appearance, function or both to the original thing or concept. A good symbol must be the simplest possible depiction.

The sky god Indra was known as an unpredictable creator and destroyer of nature. His rages, the droughts and the floods, were known to destroy crops and human dwellings. His blessings, the rain, was followed by all-around new growth of vegetation, fishes, frogs, earthworms, insects, etc. Rain was believed to bless life to every living creature. After long observation, priests formulated that the rain showers by god Indra sowed the seeds of new plants and animals.

Priests also knew that the male phallus sowed the seed of a child in a female. Phallus was the only object known to them, which was capable of giving birth to new life. Since the shower of the sky god Indra created new life as the phallus did, the wise priests deemed the phallus to be the best symbol of Indra.

It is likely that Hindu priests advised people to worship Indra through an easily carved stone sculpture of phallus called Lingam. During ancient times, the worship of phallus was universal, but it still survives in Hinduism. Thus, the stone idol of Lingam represents the creative power of Indra the sky god, not the human organ.

After invention of solar discs and Lingam, Hindu priests named the sun and the sky as Vishnu and Shiva, respectively. Gradually, people forgot the relation of these two new gods with their older versions. Gradually, Lingam became the symbol of sky god Shiva.

Shiva is the most worshipped god of modern Hindus. Shiva is still worshipped through the stone Lingam. It is debatable when Hindus associated the stone Lingam with Lord Shiva. Worship of Lingam is certainly an older concept than the name Shiva. The name of Shiva rarely appeared in the Rig Veda.

In fact, names such as Shiva, Shambhu and Shankara appeared for the first time in the Yajur Veda as different names of Indra the sky god. The *Shvetashvatara Upanishad* also narrated the new names of Indra such as Shiva, Shambhu, Shankara, Mahapurusha, Bhagavat and Maheshvara. In all these scriptures, Indra the Shiva has been described as the ultimate creator and destroyer of nature.

In the fourth century, Greek visitor Megasthenes wrote that worship of Shiva was popular during the reign of Chandragupta Maurya. The epic Mahabharata mentions, 'Upamanyu says to Krishna that Shiva is the only god whose Lingam was worshipped ('Anushasana Parva', Chapter 14).' The scripture further mentions that the other great gods such as Brahma and Vishnu also worship the Lingam; therefore, Shiva is the greatest God.

For a long period, Shiva the sky god was worshipped through the Lingam only. Later, Shiva was personified as a man. Shiva gradually metamorphosed to his recognizably human form. After this, the original concept of Shiva, the sky god, was consigned to oblivion.

Shiva was depicted as a meditating male ascetic. Priest wrote allegories about his life and marriage. The earliest depiction of Shiva, as a meditating male, can be seen in the Elephanta Cave temple. The temple was built in the sixth century CE. It had a huge monolithic Lingam and a three-headed idol of Shiva. Gradually, people improved idols of Shiva and included his modern attributes such as a trident, snakes, a river, a drum, etc. Till today, Shiva is frequently worshiped in the shape of the Lingam. The Lingam is offered milk, sweets, water, fresh flowers, fruits and tender leaves.

Not only did the priests personify the sky god, they also personified the sun as Vishnu. Lord Vishnu's name also appears in the Rig Veda but rarely. The scripture mentions that Vishnu crossed the earth, the ocean and the heavens in three strides. The sun was a known celestial object travelling that long distance daily. One hymn has depicted Vishnu as if clothed in sunlight. Various incarnations of Vishnu are not mentioned in the Rig Veda. This indicates that its poets had not yet conceived the sun god Vishnu in human shape. In fact, Vishnu was one of the several names of the sun till the Rig Veda was written. Personification of Vishnu as a male was done around a millennium later.

Much ancient evidence attests that worship of the idols of Vishnu began around 2,200 years ago. Initially, Vishnu was depicted as a huge bird called Garuda. The bird represented the vehicle of Vishnu (the sun) for its daily journey from east to west. The earliest depiction of Garuda is situated in Besnagar (Madhya Pradesh). Heliodorus, a Greek ambassador, erected this stone column that depicts a Garuda at its top. The sculpture was carved around 2,200 years ago.

Later, Vishnu was portrayed as a man sailing on a python in the sea. This depiction was to exhibit that Vishnu, the sun, took rest at night. The Dashavatara temple is the earliest surviving temple of Vishnu. It was constructed in the sixth century at Deogarh in Jhansi. The temple has an idol of Vishnu resting on a python.

A human idol of Vishnu was one of the earliest attempts to represent god as a person. Priests propagated that god Vishnu has been born in many incarnations on the earth many times. Various incarnations (avatars) of Vishnu were introduced for the first time in the *Vishnu Purana*. The book proclaims that god Vishnu took birth many times on the earth to eradicate sinners and the miseries of the masses.

This was the period when Jews also began to believe that a prophet or an incarnation of God would appear on the earth to help ease the suffering of humanity. In fact, during this period, diseases, inequality, exploitation and crimes – the result of civilization – had engulfed farmers worldwide. Therefore, the masses helplessly looked for some messiah to come and rescue them.

There were different opinions regarding the number of incarnations of Vishnu. The *Matsya Purana* mentions ten incarnations of Vishnu: fish, tortoise, boar, man-lion, dwarf, Parasurama, Rama, Krishna, the Buddha and Kalki (the future incarnation). The *Bhagavata Purana* increased this number to twenty-two; another scripture cited thirty-nine. A few more enthusiastic writers claimed the number to be in thousands and thus made a mockery of the concept. Not only were the numbers faulty, there were also many other loopholes in the theory.

For example, all incarnations of Vishnu except the Buddha were supposed to have been born before the Rig Veda was written. For example, Rama and Krishna were believed to have been born between 3000 and 1500 BCE. The poets of the Rig Veda, in 1400 BCE, did not mention Rama and Krishna. Had they been historical incarnations, the Vedic poets would not have ignored them. They must have composed at least a few flattering hymns for both these legends.

In fact, the theory of incarnations of Vishnu appeared in Hindu scriptures only after the popularity of Buddhist literature. These described many previous births of the Buddha. Historians believe that Hindu priests took the idea of incarnations from Buddhist literature.

The only definite historical incarnate of Vishnu was the Buddha. There is much evidence to prove that he existed. Surprisingly, no Vedic priest could identify the Buddha as the incarnation of Vishnu in his lifetime. Rather, he was the biggest enemy of the priests. The Buddha was against Vedic sacrifices and rituals made to appease the gods and ultimately the priests. His lesson of non-violence was also contradictory to the other incarnations.

For example, Krishna, another incarnation of Vishnu, advised his disciple Arjuna to fight with members of his own family. Had the Buddha been an adviser of Arjuna in the battle of the Mahabharata, his message would have been different. Krishna was portrayed as a lover; the Buddha was an ascetic. The attributes of the Buddha had no similarity with any other incarnation of the god Vishnu.

In fact, the Buddha was the most popular man during that time. King Ashok popularized his teachings all over India. By the time the Puranas were written, the Buddha was widely accepted as a god in human shape. It is likely that writers of the *Vishnu Purana* purposely included the Buddha in the list of incarnations of the god Vishnu.

This declaration must have achieved three objectives: Vedic priests cashed in on the popularity of the Buddha as god; they authenticated their incarnation theory by adding a known historical man; and they attracted many Buddhists to the worship of Vishnu.

Apart from the male deities, many female deities were worshipped in almost all ancient civilizations. Similarly, in the Indian subcontinent, the concept of the female deity began around five thousand years ago in the Indus Valley. During the Vedic period a goddess of fertility called Prithvi was worshipped. Around 2,200 years ago, Hindus began to worship a female goddess called Shakti. Later, many local female deities were worshipped. Durga, Devi, Kali and Chandi were different names of the goddess Shakti. Gradually, people began to worship the consorts of almost all male gods. Hindus still worship female goddesses regularly.

Thus, the period between 300 BCE and 300 CE witnessed the personification of Vedic gods. Now, people worshipped the sun and the sky as Vishnu and Shiva respectively. Besides, people also worshipped the Buddha, Mahavira, and Shakti. Contemporary masses follow all the faiths but priests prefer sectarian labels such as Buddhist, Vaishnava, Shaiva, and Shakta.

This period witnessed an upsurge in the field of literature; several Puranas and the two legendry epics were written during this period. Gradually, these scriptures shaped Hinduism. The most popular deities of present-day Hinduism, Krishna and Ram, were introduced by the epics, the Mahabharata and the Ramayana respectively. Eminent historian and author Romila Thapar has written: 'Epics are not histories, but are again a way of looking at the past.'

During that period, books were written on plant leaves, which necessitated copying them regularly for their survival. It was not an easy job; many priests wrote round the year. Every new copying provided writers with the opportunity to reform and interpolate. Historians believe that the original poets of the Ramayana and the Mahabharata wrote secular literature. Later, interpolations during copying by generations of priests promoted both the epics to a divine status.

The Ramayana was written in Sanskrit by Valmiki. Most historians assert that Valmiki wrote the Ramayana around 2,300 years ago. Many historians believe that the story probably reflects a poetic exaggeration of some historical war between the kings of the north and those of the south. Some others believe that Valmiki wrote fiction and depicted Ram as its hero. Fiction seems a more likely possibility since the time period of the birth of Ram is a subject of great discrepancy among historians. Some historians believe that Ram and Valmiki lived in the same time period – around 2,300 years ago. There are many who believe that Ram took birth in the pre-Vedic period. Social, political and personal state of affairs described in the Ramayana corresponds to the period of its writing, not to the pre-Vedic era.

Many characters of the Ramayana were idealistic representatives of their roles. For example, Ram was an ideal human, son, brother, husband and king. He ruled over a big empire and performed an Ashvamedha Yajna. At one place, the Ramayana mentions that Ram was advised to worship the sun as a common man. In fact, Valmiki depicted Ram as an ideal king and a great human being, not as a god. Only a few stanzas described Ram as an incarnation of Vishnu. Historians believe that these were later interpolations.

Another great epic, the Mahabharata, was the longest and the best among other contemporary literary works in the world. Historians believe that the original poet began composing the Mahabharata from the fourth century BCE and additions continued till the fourth century CE. Again, the original script of the Mahabharata was secular; none of its original characters was a deity. Later, Bhagavad Gita and *Harivamsa* introduced the divine character of Krishna in it. Krishna was portrayed as an incarnation of the sun god Vishnu, who took birth to control the deteriorating law and order situation on the earth.

Later literature depicted Krishna as a universal lover. In the twelfth century, Jayadeva immortalized the love of Radha and Krishna through his book *Geeta Govinda*. He described the moments of love between Krishna and Radha in an erotic language. Today, Krishna is the most worshipped Hindu god.

According to the Mahabharata, Krishna was born around 5,000 years ago in Mathura. Archaeologists have attested that inhabitation of Mathura began only three thousand years ago. There is no evidence of any ruined palace or the capital of a king. Besides, there is no evidence of the famous war as well. Around 2,000 years ago, Mathura was the centre of the Buddhist and the Jain religions. During that time, the Mathura School of Art developed and artists made many idols of Mahavira, the Buddha, contemporary kings and other local deities, but they did not carve a single sculpture of Krishna.

The Bhagavad Gita, the most important part of the Mahabharata, is usually considered a separate book. It was written between the first and the third century CE. It was a compilation of lessons taught by Krishna to Arjuna, the hero of the Mahabharata. The teachings of the Gita are at the core of all Hindu philosophy till date and supposed to be followed by all devotees. Modern worshippers of Krishna sing and enjoy many love songs of Krishna. They believe that singing the glory of Krishna will give them his blessings. The teachings of the Gita can be summarized as follows:

Why do you worry?
Whom do you fear?

> Who can kill you?
> Your death is a new birth for another life.
> Your body is not yours.
> It is made of water, air and soil.
> After death, the body will convert to these elements.
> But your soul is for eternity, neither born nor dead.
> Your body is like a temporary dress of the soul.
> Death only destroys your body.
> Your soul remains alive forever.
> Nature is ever-changing.
> Have no regrets for the past.
> The present is good, and the future will be bright.
> Did you bring anything with you when you were born?
> You came empty-handed.
> You cannot lose anything,
> since you brought nothing when you were born.
> What belongs to you today
> belonged to someone else yesterday.
> It will go to someone else tomorrow.
> You are miserable because you love your possessions.
> Devote yourself to God, which is the only way
> to get rid of fear, worries and all other miseries.

The period from the fourth to the sixth centuries CE, i.e. the Gupta period, was the golden period of Hinduism. The Gupta kings gave state patronage to all the prevailing faiths, namely, Buddhism, Jainism, Vaishnavism and Shaivism. During this period, India witnessed a great upsurge in the fields of science, literature and arts. It was exceptional and far ahead of the rest of the world.

For example, Arya Bhatta calculated the value of 'pi' as 3.1416 and the length of the year as 365.358 days. For the first time in the world, Arya Bhatta discovered that the earth was a huge ball that revolved on its axis and rotated round the sun. He studied and wrote details of solar and lunar eclipses. Around one millennium later,

Western scientists Copernicus and Galileo could recognize the fact that the earth revolved round the sun.

The Gupta kings also promoted poets such as Kalidasa and Bhavabhuti. Panini and Patanjali wrote the rules of grammar. Ayurveda, the system of herbal remedies, also developed in this period. Several herbal remedies were invented, which are still relevant and widely practised today. Practices of sanitation, such as washing hands and bathing, were promoted as holy duties in view of their efficacy in preventing diseases. Patanjali wrote *Yoga Sutra*, containing details of yogic exercises and philosophy. Many ascetics practised the yogic exercises to keep themselves physically fit and to have transcendental experiences. Almost all the other religions also invented sanitation but only Hinduism discovered specific exercises to keep oneself healthy.

This period witnessed exploration of human sexuality also. The Kama Sutra was an exceptional work in that regard. Contemporary priests considered the sexual act as sacred and a method of inducing trances. At some places, they depicted sexual postures on the exterior of temple walls. Idol worship was firmly established during this age, though it originated earlier. The Gupta period witnessed a steep rise in the development of temple architecture.

Hindus began solar worship in the Vedic period, but it was prevalent even after the Gupta period. Around 1,400 years ago, astrologer Varahamihira wrote the ritual ceremonies to install the idol of the sun god. A century later, poet Mayura, during the reign of King Harshvardhana, wrote a poem to glorify the sun god. He advised people to worship the sun.

King Harshavardhana worshipped all the gods regularly in public functions. He organized a meeting at Allahabad that continued for many days. He worshipped the Buddha on the first day, Surya/Vishnu the sun god on the second day, and Shiva the sky god on the third day. Xuan Zang, who visited India during this period, also mentioned the popularity of the Buddha, Surya/Vishnu and Shiva. Iran was a well-known centre of solar worship at that time, and priests from Iran visited India to officiate at ceremonies of sun worship.

Solar worship was prevalent in India till medieval times. For example, Martanda and Katarmal Surya temple in the north, Suryanaar Koyil in the south, Konark on the east coast and Modhera in western India are concrete evidence of the solar cult. These temples were constructed around one millennium ago. The temples were not confined to one region but existed all over India, including Pakistan. This indicates a widespread solar cult. Almost all the antique Hindu temples were dedicated to the sun god.

At the end of the eighth century CE, Hindus worshipped Vishnu the sun god, Shiva the sky god, Shakti and many local gods. Priests and devotees were known by the name of the god they worshipped. During this time, Adi Shankara, the first Hindu reformer, initiated a marathon effort to organize different sects of Hindus. He advocated the philosophy of Advaita, which literally means something unique. He advocated that there exists one and only one God who can be called by any name. Knowledge leads to understanding of God.

Adi Shankara debated with many philosophers and convinced them of his viewpoint. He travelled almost all over India and unified various sects among Hindus. He built four temples, the Mathas, in four corners of India like state capitals. Today, the heads of these Mathas are called Shankaracharyas; they are considered the ultimate Hindu religious authorities.

Around this time, Hindus began another kind of devotional worship called Bhakti. Poets composed several flattering songs to glorify Vishnu and Shiva in south India and later throughout the entire country. People sung these songs repeatedly. The first literary work containing devotional songs was written in the sixth century by Karaikkal Ammaiyar. She wrote songs in Tamil to glorify Shiva.

By the end of the ninth century CE, Hindu devotees began singing many flattering songs for Vishnu and Shiva all over India. Vishnu was now worshipped as his human incarnation Krishna, and Shiva was considered as a male ascetic. By this time, people began to organize kirtans – the singing of devotional songs publicly. Kirtan was a form of musical group worship practised by both the Shaivas and the Vaishnavas. During kirtan, one main singer sung the song loudly with music and the people repeated after him.

In the eleventh century CE, Ramanujan taught that bhakti was the only way to please gods. Kirtan was further popularized by the Bengali mystic Chaitanya (1468–1534CE). Chaitanya taught worship of Krishna through music and dance. The trend of singing and dancing for gods swept throughout India and continued for centuries to come. Later other bhakti poets such as Tulsidas and Mira Bai exalted the bhakti movement. Kabir Das tried his best to enlighten people about the universality and oneness of God. He argued that crying aloud for God is futile, as God is not deaf. It is best therefore to worship God in solitude and peace without the mediation of priests.

Kirtan is still one of the popular modes of group worship. Today, it is done with great fanfare. Today, most of the kirtan songs are dedicated to Krishna and he is portrayed as a charming man who attracts both males and females. Singers invite Krishna to meet them at least once. They express that the only purpose of their life is to meet Krishna. In fact, kirtan music is relaxing, often bringing a sense of ecstasy to the listeners, which people often misunderstand as a divine presence.

In the sixteenth century CE, Guru Nanak (1469–1539CE) founded Sikhism, an altogether new kind of Bhakti or devotional movement. Nanak took birth in an educated merchant family, in the province of Punjab. Since his childhood he was exceptionally intelligent and inclined to excavate the truth about different gods.

He studied scriptures of almost all the religions prevalent in India. He visited many temples, shrines and mosques. He put forth many questions to all the religious teachers he met, but was disappointed with their answers.

At the age of thirty-eight, Nanak had an epiphany. It is said that God himself spoke to Guru Nanak and asked him to repeat His name and motivate others to do so. God said, 'Live in purity, repeat My name, do charity, do worship and do meditation.' In fact, Sikhism was reformation and unification of many religious concepts prevalent among contemporary Indian masses. Guru Nanak founded an altogether new religion by assimilation of various concepts he liked from different religions. He adopted certain moral lessons from the Buddha, the mode of worship such as kirtans and rituals from Hindus and the concept of God from Muslims.

Nanak taught that there is one and only one God. Anyone can receive His blessings through devotion and good deeds. Guru Arjun Dev, the fifth guru, compiled the teachings of Nanak and many other Hindu and Muslim preachers in a huge book. This sacred book is called Guru Granth Sahib, and Sikhs consider this as the prime object of worship and following.

After Nanak, a great poet Tulsidas (1532–1623ce) gave a new impetus to the bhakti movement. Tulsidas translated the great epic of Ramayana into Hindi naming it *Ramcharitmanas*. The book is a great work of poetry. Tulsidas described Ram as an incarnation of god Vishnu. He mentioned that Ram was a contemporary of the poet Valmiki. Tulsidas emphasized that Sita, the wife of Ram, herself narrated an eyewitness account of the story to the poet. The sons of Ram and Sita were born in Valmiki's ashram. The capital of Ram's kingdom was Ayodhya, a small town in eastern Uttar Pradesh. Ayodhya had no architecture that can be recognized as Ram's palace. Besides, excavation of the city does not evince any proof of such a palace.

Fa-Hien, a Chinese pilgrim who visited Ayodhya in the fifth century, wrote that he found around one hundred Buddhist monasteries in Ayodhya, but mentioned no palace or temple of Ram. In fact, almost all the temples of Ram were constructed after Tulsidas. The most ancient temple of Rama is in Karnataka, built in the sixteenth century CE. Ram temple at Kumbakonam in Tamil Nadu was constructed in the seventeenth century CE.

In fact, Tulsidas translated the age-old fiction in the popular Hindi language, labelling it as history. It was Tulsidas who introduced Ram, Sita and Hanuman as deities for the first time. Tulsidas wrote an allegory and glorified Ram as an incarnate of god Vishnu. King Ram was widely worshipped as a god only after this book was written. *Ramcharitmanas* was so popular in India that the British considered it as the Bible of the Hindus.

Hinduism suffered a major setback in the late nineteenth century when Indian and Western scholars explored the Vedic texts. In 1884, linguist Friedrich Max Muller was appointed by the British government to translate the Rig Veda into English. In this process he discovered that the Sanskrit, Latin, Persian and Greek languages had a few common words. Scholars thought that people speaking similar words must have been related sometime. They might have common ancestors. Therefore, some people might have come from some other country in India.

Max Muller and other historians suggested that around 4,000 years ago, a fair-skinned race migrated from Central Asia to Europe and Iran. Later, a few groups from the Iranian migrants also invaded India. These invaders were considered to be Arya – the poets of the Rig Veda. The British called them the Aryans.

The hypothesis was accepted for a century by many historians. They discussed the origin, time, and path of the Aryans for a hundred years. But now, many historians believe that the Aryans were indigenous to the Indian subcontinent and lived in western India around Punjab.

New historians argue that the theory of Aryan invasion has no archaeological evidence. Anthropologist Edmund Leach said in 1990: 'The Aryan invasion never happened.' Furthermore, the poets of the Rig Veda also have not mentioned any story of their long migratory journey.

Apart from these, the Aryan invasion theory has many other loopholes. For example, Aryans migrated to Iran first and then to India; but they wrote the Rig Veda only in India – their last destination. Western scholars propagated that the Aryans came to India with the words and hymns of the Rig Veda. Obviously, the Aryans that stayed back in Iran also had knowledge of similar hymns. In that case, they too would have written at least a few hymns of the Rig Veda in their language.

For example, the Gayatri mantra was composed around five thousand years ago, well before the so-called Aryan race started entering India. According to Max Muller, the Aryans must have come chanting the Gayatri mantra all the way. Obviously, the leftover Aryans in Iran must have been chanting the hymn regularly. Ancient Iranian literatures had no similar hymns. No other Indo-European race had any literary work earlier than the Rig Veda. The earliest literary work of the Iranians, the Avesta, was written much later. In the Rig Veda the word 'Deva' is used for god and 'Asura' for demon. On the contrary, in Avesta, 'Ahura' is god and 'Daeva' means evil demon.

Thus, there are many reasons to believe that the Aryans, the aforesaid foreigners, were in fact indigenous priests who wrote the Rig Veda. Probably some Indian priests might have migrated from India to Iran and Europe with the knowledge of Sanskrit. They must have added a few words of Sanskrit to the native languages.

8

Judaism

Judaism – the seed of all the monotheistic faiths – sprouted in the sacred land of Jerusalem. It was the first monotheist religion of the world. Its history is best documented in the Old Testament – the Bible of Jews. Christianity and Islam also attest many stories of the Old Testament. The first book of the Jewish Bible is Genesis, which narrates how God created all the animals and plants on the earth.

According to the Bible, God created the world in six days. On the first two days, God manufactured media prima – the raw material of living beings. On the third day, God grew all the plants on the face of the earth. On the fourth and fifth days, He created all the animals in the shapes seen today. On the sixth day, God crafted the first man – Adam. The same day, He took the twelfth rib of Adam and fashioned it into the first female – Eve. On the seventh day, being exhausted, He rested.

Today, this theory is the most elaborate, interesting and widely accepted belief about the origin of life on the earth. Not only Jews, but Christians and Muslims also believe this biblical theory of special creation. The Bible mentions that God created man in his own image: obviously God was a man. The book mentions that the first prophet was Noah. He was a direct descendant of Adam and Eve. He was the first man to receive messages from God. Noah was probably a worshipper of the sky god of Mesopotamia who was responsible for rain. At one point in time, God said to Noah, 'The earth is filled with violence and, behold, I will destroy them. Soon, one massive Flood will engulf the earth, and you should make an Ark.'

At the time of the Flood, Noah was an exceptional old man of 600 years. He prepared an Ark. God inflicted the Flood that drowned all the sinners and innocent animals as well. The Flood spared only the men and animals sailing on the ark. Noah lived another 350 years. The Flood is also documented in the stone tablets excavated in Mesopotamia. In fact, this area is situated between two rivers. It is almost sure that at some point in time, the area faced a massive flood that gave rise to the myth.

Noah's family was the only family that survived the Flood. Their offspring gave birth to mankind all over the world. After the Flood, Noah's family settled in Babylonia. They built good houses and the Tower of Babel.

Once, God came down to see the city and the tower. God said, 'Behold, the people are one, and they have one language; and by this they may begin to do anything; and no one can restrain them. Go to the earth and confound their language, that they may not understand one another's speech.'

It is surprising that God who advised people to love each other also divided them intentionally. The story propagates that the achievements of men annoyed God enough to confound their languages. He tried to divide them and rule like a politician. The Jewish Bible depicts God as a person who was jealous of the achievements of men.

It appears that the authors of the Bible had some different motive behind this particular language theory. During that time, people of different locales spoke different languages. The authors had to explain why people of the world – the children of Adam and Eve – spoke different languages. They must have written the theory to explain the diversity of languages. These authors wisely explained that at one point in time God himself had confounded the languages.

After Noah, the Bible talks about prophet Abraham. Around four thousand years ago, Abraham initiated the Jewish religion in Israel and adjoining areas. The Bible narrates that Abraham was a direct descendant of Noah. Initially, he lived in Mesopotamia. At one point in time, God commanded him: 'Get thee out of thy country, and from thy kindred, and from thy father's house, unto a land that I will show thee.' Abraham followed God's order. He travelled a distance of around seven hundred kilometres on foot along with his relatives and cattle.

Historians believe that Abraham had to leave Mesopotamia because of some famine. On his way, he stayed in Egypt where the king welcomed him. The king fell in love with Abraham's sixty-year-old beautiful wife Sarah and wished to possess her. Soon, the watchful God sent a plague to punish the king for violating moral values.

Abraham finally settled in the area of modern Israel but he had no child. After some time, he asked God, 'You ordered me to settle in a fertile land, but who would inherit this land? Kindly bless me with a child.' God ordered Abraham to sacrifice four animals. Soon, Abraham sacrificed the desired animals. Immediately after the slaughter, the happy God promised to give him a child and made a covenant with him.

God tried to bless him with a child but his wife Sarah was too old to conceive. Sarah herself persuaded Abraham to mate with her Egyptian maid Hagar to produce a baby. Hagar gave birth to Ishmael and obliged Abraham when he was eighty-six years old. After the birth of her stepson, Sarah again felt depressed. Muslims believe themselves to be descendants of Ishmael.

When Abraham was ninety years old, God again appeared before him and said that Abraham would be father of many nations. Now, Abraham again asked God to bless him with a son through Sarah. God asked for a peculiar sacrifice: the foreskin of every male. Abraham ordered all the males to sacrifice their foreskin – thereby initiating the practice of circumcision. The elderly Abraham along with other males of his family were circumcised. After His wish was fulfilled, God promised to Abraham that soon Sarah would bear his son.

God personally came to Abraham and Sarah to fulfil His promise. The couple welcomed God and offered him butter, milk and a recently dressed calf. God ate these while sitting under a tree. God asked Abraham, 'Where is Sarah, thy wife?' Abraham said, 'Behold, in the tent.' Sarah laughed at the impossible promise of God.

Abraham was also dubious whether the old lady would conceive. God said to Sarah, 'Is anything too difficult for the Lord?' While leaving, God said to Sarah, 'Shall I hide from Abraham that thing which I do?' Sometime after this meeting with God, Abraham was surprised to see Sarah pregnant. At the age of ninety, Sarah gave birth to a male child, Isaac. Jews believe that they are descendants of Isaac.

Later, when Isaac became an adolescent, God ordered Abraham to take his only son and burn him as a sacrifice. God said, 'Take now thy son, your only son Isaac, whom you love, and go to the region of Moriah; and offer him there as a burnt offering upon one of the mountains, which I would tell you.'

Abraham packed for the journey taking his son with him and reached the place in three days. There he built an altar by the woods, laid his son upon it, and took a big knife to slay his son. In the nick of time, Abraham heard the voice of an angel of God, from the sky: 'Here I am; do not slay your son.' Suddenly, a ram appeared before Abraham, and he took it to the altar and sacrificed it.

Abraham was the earliest prophet of all the three monotheistic faiths. Historians have debated much about Abraham's God. It has been stated in the Bible that Abraham had not heard the name of the Jewish god Yahweh. Evidence indicates that Abraham probably worshipped the sky god.

Exodus is another book of the Jewish Bible. At one point in time, the Egyptian king enslaved many Israelites, the Jews. Exodus is the story of the liberation of the Israelite slaves from Egypt. Exodus contains the most important story and teachings of the Jewish religion. In the beginning, it describes the sufferings of the Israelites. In later chapters, the book narrates the story of Moses – the most important prophet of Jews.

It is believed that Moses was born around three thousand years ago. Before the birth of Moses, the Egyptian king ordered that all male newborns of Israelite slaves must be killed. At that time, the mother of Moses was pregnant and she wished to save her child after its birth. After the birth of Moses, she placed the child in a basket and allowed it to float down the Nile River. An Egyptian queen rescued the child and named him Moses. After the boy grew up, he noticed the exploitation of the Israelite slaves by the Egyptians. Later, Moses discovered that he was an Israelite, so he decided to rescue his people.

Exodus narrates how God appeared before Moses. One day, Moses saw a burning bush; he took it to be a divine presence. Other books of the Bible such as Deuteronomy mention, God's meeting with Moses in a different way:

> Moses heard the voice of God: 'Collect the people to hear My words, that they may learn to fear Me all the days that they shall live upon the earth, and that they may teach their children.' People came and stood under the mountain. The mountain burned with fire unto the midst of heaven with darkness, clouds and thick darkness. God spoke out from the midst of fire; people heard the voice, but could not see God.

In fact, before Moses, the Israelites worshipped Baal – the god of the thunderstorm. Moses saw clouds, darkness and fire (lightning) between the mountain and the sky. He heard the frightening voice, but did not see the face. It is likely that the meeting of God with Moses was a severe storm. The strong thunder was interpreted by Moses to be the voice of God.

God appeared before Moses again. Moses heard a voice from the sky: 'I am the God of Abraham, Isaac and Jacob. I am aware of the atrocities on the Israelites in Egypt. I will send you to the king, and you shall free my people, the Israelites, from Egypt.' Moses replied, 'Who am I to do that difficult job?' God said, 'I will be with you for that.' Moses was surprised and asked the name of the voice, which replied: 'I am that I am.'

Exodus further mentions that Moses again met his God. Moses asked God, 'Why will the Pharaoh listen to me?' God immediately showed a feat of magic: He turned a stick into a snake. Frightened, Moses looked towards the sky for help, and God changed the snake back into a stick.

After this event, Moses discovered that he had been gifted with divine powers to do extraordinary things. He could now change water into blood and vice versa. Moses was now confident enough to fight the king. Since he stammered, he asked God for a spokesman. Aaron, his brother, was a good orator; he was appointed to help Moses immediately.

Chapter six of Exodus narrates that Moses again heard the voice and asked his name. The voice replied: 'I am Yahweh, I am the same God that your ancestors Abraham, Isaac and Jacob worshipped, but they did not know my divine name.' Moses was thus the first prophet to declare that he had received a revelation of the Jewish God Yahweh. He declared that he had been chosen to lead the children of Israel out of Egypt.

Chapter seven of Exodus explains that Moses and Aaron go to

the Pharaoh and request him to release the Hebrew slaves. The king refuses. Moses says that his God Yahweh desires it, but the king refuses to recognize his God. Then Moses exhibits his supernatural power by turning a stick into a snake. The king calls his magician who shows the same magical feat to Moses. The king rejects all their demands. Moses tries to convince him that it was his God Yahweh who had sent all previous plagues to Egypt and threatens the king with further plagues. The angry king orders his men to inflict more atrocities upon the Hebrew slaves.

The next chapter of Exodus details the ten plagues inflicted by Yahweh on the Egyptians. The following were the plagues:

Plague One: The waters of the Nile turned blood red.
Plague Two: An abnormal number of frogs originated.
Plagues Three and Four: Attacks of different insects.
Plague Five: An epidemic.
Plague Six: A skin disease.
Plague Seven: A destructive storm.
Plague Eight: An attack of locusts.
Plague Nine: Profound darkness (probably a solar eclipse).
Plague Ten: Death of the firstborn.

Many Jews argued that these plagues hurt them as well. Therefore, Moses advised them to sacrifice a lamb and mark their doorpost with its blood. During the tenth plague, Yahweh sent the angel of death who passed over the houses with the mark of the lamb blood and spared their firstborn.

At last, the Exodus mentions that one day Yahweh himself came to liberate the enslaved Jews. He took the Jews to the Red Sea. Soldiers of the king of Egypt followed the Jews. Yahweh made a way through the middle of the Red Sea for the Jews, but drowned the Egyptians who were following. The story leaves the impression that Yahweh was not kind. God instructed Moses to celebrate the liberation of the Israelites as the festival of Passover.

Exodus is said to be the history of the period around three thousand years ago. In fact, Moses must have noticed the sufferings of the Israelites; so he organized them for their freedom. He advised them to worship only God Yahweh. Moses declared that Yahweh had sent many plagues to kill the Egyptians. Moses could only organize the Jews by propagating that the most powerful God is behind them. Judaism was the first organized religion of the world. It was essentially a mass movement under the leadership of Moses and the banner of the plague-causing God Yahweh.

The Bible further mentions that Moses was atop a hill for a few months with God, and returned with the Ten Commandments. In those times there existed no rules of the state; people followed only what they believed to be the divine rules. It is likely that Moses took several months to make moral laws and write them on stone. To implement these laws effectively, he declared these laws to have been conveyed to him by God. The Ten Commandments have been mentioned earlier in Chapter 6.

Similar to other religions, the Jewish priests also found explanations as to why many immoral people were happy and several honest ones suffered. The priests propagated that every individual suffers or enjoys the outcome of his own deeds. Handwritten copies of the Torah, the Hebrew laws and doctrines, are aesthetically decorated in synagogues, the Jewish temples. Traditional Jews follow the Torah in its entirety and believe that its teachings should not be changed. The less traditional Jews believe that the teachings of the Torah can be adapted to suit the needs of modern life.

Jews conceived their God Yahweh as a human being, but an immortal one. Once you assume God to be human, he has to have human evils as well, such as discrimination and cruelty. The Jews were aware that God could set a forest on fire and destroy it, send floods, and shake the earth when He wished. Whenever He expressed

His anger by sending calamities such as epidemics, Jewish priests appeased Him by the sacrifice of a tribesman or animal.

After reading the Exodus, it is obvious that God Yahweh regularly visited prophet Moses. Every time, Yahweh threatened the people with death for violating the Ten Commandments. Moses propagated the command and wish of Yahweh to the people. Yahweh wished that the people only worship Him. After the death of Moses, God Yahweh never visited the earth.

Sacrifice was an essential and elaborately prescribed part of Judaism. Almost all the prayers to Yahweh began with burnt and other sacrifices. It is said that ancient Jews sacrificed their first child because they believed that childbirth reduced God's energy. It surprises one today that people could consider restoring the power of almighty God through killing a child.

Let us consider why Jews killed animals as a sacrifice to appease Yahweh. Did Yahweh enjoy the animal sacrifice as a sport? Did he eat them? It is far more likely that Jews killed animals only in order to eat them. Yahweh had nothing to do with the hunger of Jews or the suffering of the innocent animals. Mankind did whatever they wished, liked or required, not necessarily by divine sanction as most religious scriptures propagate.

Discussion on the stories of the Bible leads us to the conclusion that these were simply myths of the time. People believed that someone in the sky caused their sufferings, such as plagues, storms, earthquakes or epidemics. Moses simply named that sky power Yahweh. As these were documented, later people believed these fables to be historical facts.

All pagan religions had many gods, so the followers were always ready to accept new gods. Judaism being a monotheistic religion, message of its God was: I am the only God; worship no other gods but me. This doctrine of 'no other gods' meant denying all other faiths. Many followers of Judaism and its daughter religions committed violence only to enforce this doctrine.

9

Christianity

Two thousand years ago, Jesus planted a twig from the tree of Judaism in Palestine. Today, the twig has grown into a big tree called Christianity. It is the most widely practised religion today. Around one-third of the earth's population is Christian. Historians know little about the early life of Jesus.

The Bible of the Christians, the New Testament, was written about forty years after the death of Jesus. It was originally written in Greek, not in Aramaic – the language spoken by Jesus and his disciples. After 1,300 years, the Bible was translated into English. The Bible has many books named after their authors: Matthew, Mark, Luke, John, etc. The authors have written about the life story, teachings and miracles of Jesus.

According to the Bible, the angel Gabriel visited a virgin named Mary, and told her that she had been chosen to bear the Son of God. Thus, Mary gave birth to Jesus by the miraculous gift of God. The exact year of his birth is not known. He must have taken birth within three years of his popularly accepted year of birth — the zero year of the Gregorian calendar. Historians believe that Jesus was the son of Joseph and Mary of Nazareth, a town near Jerusalem.

Even during adolescence, Jesus was a thoughtful boy and preferred to participate in philosophical discussions rather than play boyish games. His parents took him to the synagogue of Jerusalem at the age of twelve.

Jesus initiated his career as a faith healer in Nazareth, his home town. The Bible presents Jesus as a common man except that he had divine powers to heal the sick and forgive sinners. At the age of thirty, he met John the Baptist on the banks of the Jordan River. Later, John became the spiritual teacher of Jesus. John had a strong belief in the biblical prediction of the birth of the Messiah. He persuaded the people to take a bath in the river Jordan to purify them. This purification was called baptism.

The Bible narrates the baptizing of Jesus by John. It mentions: 'After bathing, Jesus straightaway came out of the water; he saw the Heavens opened and a spirit descending on him like a dove. A voice from heaven said, "Thou art my beloved Son, with whom I am well pleased." After viewing this scene, John designated Jesus as the Messiah.'

After his baptism, Jesus went to a secluded desert. He fasted for forty days and forty nights. As a result of his deep meditation, his body got a new spiritual strength.

After this episode, Jesus returned to his native place and began to treat patients through his divine powers similar to other priests of the time. He also taught many moral lessons to the people. After hearing him, they became his followers and began to consider Jesus as their saviour. The Sermon on the Mount is the collection of his teachings. He sent twelve devotees in different directions to spread his teachings.

During the lifetime of Jesus, priest-doctors or faith healers were regarded as gods. In fact, they were the priest, teacher, doctor and magician, all in one. By then, people had adopted cultivation almost all over the globe. It has already been discussed how cultivation, population explosion and domestication exposed men to many deadly infectious diseases. People suffered from tuberculosis, cholera, plague and many other diseases.

In that age, humanity underwent the worst kind of suffering and average life expectancy was very short. The mortality rate of mothers and infants was high. Besides, the masses wrestled with poverty, exploitation and crimes. These unexplained human sufferings promoted priest-doctors or faith healers to the status of gods.

Jesus worked as a faith healer in his home town Nazareth. He was famous for his miraculous way of healing. His profession gave him a divine status in society. Even during his lifetime, many people in Jerusalem believed that he had divine powers. Jesus himself admitted to possessing divine powers but never claimed to have these exclusively. He preached that anyone who had faith in God would be blessed with such powers. The Bible mentions that Jesus also performed other miracles such as exorcism, walking on water, turning water into wine and reviving the dead.

One day, Jesus went to Jerusalem temple with many followers, during the Passover festival. According to Matthew, Jesus chased the sacrificial animals away and turned the tables of the Jewish merchants at the temple. His disciples made every effort to convince the Jews that Jesus was the Messiah mentioned in the Old Testament but the Jews did not accept it. A week later, Jesus had a meeting with all his disciples. This event is known as the Last Supper.

In this last meeting, Jesus declared himself to be the Son of God. The news reached the priests of the Jews. They took it as an insult to their god. They declared him to be an atheist. During that time, the punishment for the crime of atheism was death. Soon the Sanhedrin, the supreme council, issued orders to arrest Jesus. Roman soldiers captured Jesus in the night with the help of his disciple Judas.

During the trial, the high priest asked Jesus: 'Are you the Son of God?' Jesus answered: 'You say that I am.' Jesus was convicted of atheism. The Roman general sentenced him to be crucified. After this, the Jews mocked him. They asked him to save himself from the painful death if he was the Son of God.

In the late afternoon, Jesus was nailed to a wooden cross to hang there till death. This was a common Roman punishment inflicted on political offenders, robbers and criminals. Above the head of Jesus they wrote: 'This is Jesus the King of the Jews.'

The Bible mentions that God was annoyed by the crucifixion of His son and expressed anger through a storm. That darkened the sky from noon till the death of Jesus in late afternoon. The book also records a severe earthquake that caused great damage to the temple of the Jews. Surprisingly, God did nothing to save His son from the painful death, but shook the earth and the sky later.

The body of Jesus was brought down from the cross in the evening. One of his disciples, Joseph, took the body and buried it in a tomb. On the third day, three ladies of the town were surprised to see the tomb empty. Almost all the books of the Bible mention that the disciples of Jesus saw him alive at various places of Jerusalem. The Bible mentions (Matthews 27: 64–66) that the Jewish priests already had the doubt that the disciples of Jesus may steal his corpse. Therefore, the priests ordered to keep a watch on the sepulchre.

Surprisingly, Jesus addressed no public meeting, like the Last Supper, after his famous resurrection. Many devotees claimed to have seen him after his death. The description in the Bible indicates that Jesus hid somewhere. The crucifixion was a more potent reality than the return of Jesus to life. Even today, controversies about his death and resurrection are not resolved. Some historians believe that the crucifixion injured Jesus badly, but did not kill him. Many historians believe that followers of Jesus stole his body from the tomb and later claimed to have seen him alive.

Jesus was crucified because he wished to reform Judaism. He never denounced the Jewish God Yahweh. Rather, he claimed himself to be the Son of God. Why did the Jews kill a noble man whose only crime was that he claimed to be the Son of God? God of every religion is supposed to be the father of every creature. The problem was in the fundamentalist nature of the Jews. Their obstinacy was responsible for the barbaric acts they committed. Jesus never questioned the existence of God. He just added a human element to it. Prophets of other religions had also initiated a move to abolish animal sacrifices but they were not crucified. For example, five hundred years before Jesus, the Buddha made such an effort in India. Not only sacrifices, the Buddha even denied the existence of all gods. Hindu priests did not convict him. Rather, they changed their own doctrine and abolished the practice of animal sacrifices.

In fact, Jesus was a successful priest-doctor who lived his life as a common man. Only after his death, he was designated as Christ, Prophet, Messiah or the Son of God. It was the famous resurrection that established Jesus as Christ for millennia to come.

The crucifixion of Jesus killed a noble man, but gave birth to Christ – the most popular god till date. The purpose of the crucifixion was not to kill Jesus, but to denounce him as a common man. The Jews wished to prove that he was not the Son of God. They wanted to kill only the Messiah, not Jesus. The Jews committed a grave mistake since the consequence of their act was just the opposite of what they wished. They killed Jesus and gave birth to a Messiah.

Jesus was a great person with immense foresight. His principle 'Do unto others as thou would have them do unto thee' was excellent. It sums up the message of all the religions in the least possible words.

The Bible was written about four decades after the death of Jesus. By then, historical facts were either distorted or the authors added magical events to glorify Jesus. The writers depicted Jesus as the Son of God with the help of many imaginary stories. Historians believe that most of the magical events mentioned in the Bible are not a record of actual happenings.

For example, the authors of the Bible wrote that Jesus took birth through a virgin, Mary. It was written to establish that the birth of Jesus was a divine event. Second, they had to glorify him as the Son of God. Hence, they consigned his biological father Joseph to oblivion. The belief that he was the Son of God developed only after the Bible was written. His image as a man was gradually replaced by the idea of the Son of God. People initiated the worship of Jesus a few centuries after his death. Jesus and his twelve disciples taught the people in Aramaic. Therefore, the authors of the Bible must have received the teachings of Jesus in Aramaic. Surprisingly, they wrote the Bible in Greek.

Jesus was not aware of his birthday that is celebrated today. Originally, 25 December was a popular holiday in the days of the Roman Empire. It was considered the day of the new birth of the sun (*dies solis invicti nati*). It was celebrated around the shortest day of the year – the winter solstice.

Since time immemorial, people had celebrated this day because it signified 'rebirth' to the sun – the sustainer of life. This day was a day of bright future. After this, the sun increased his blessings, i.e., its rays. In fact, during those cold days, people eagerly awaited 25 December. After this day, the weather became warmer. Gradually, the 'birthday' of the sun god became the birthday of Jesus – the Son of God. People recognized the birthday of Jesus around two hundred years after his death. Sextus Julius Africanus designated 25 December as the birthday of Jesus for the first time.

Christianity first spread to Rome. In fact, till the time of Emperor Constantine, the Romans worshiped the sun. Constantine himself became a Christian and made it the official religion of the state.

Gradually, Christianity spread to other parts of Europe, and ultimately the whole world.

During the last two thousand years, Christians ruled most of the world. They all believed that the words in the Bible were the words of God. This conviction designated the Bible as the most authentic book. Thus, the globe was ruled by the Bible for a long period. The Bible and the popes did not permit many scientific inventions which disputed their teachings.

The foray into medical science initiated by Hippocrates remained stationary for two millennia after the death of Galen. After Galen, no medical discoveries were permitted by the popes. Thus, the divine knowledge of the Bible delayed the scientific progress of the world.

The core teaching of Jesus said: 'Love all and do not kill even animals.' His last words for the people crucifying him read: 'Father forgive them; for they know not what they do.' Thus, the basic teaching of Jesus was non-violence and forgiveness. On the contrary, many devotees of Jesus rarely followed non-violence. They considered that only the killings in the temple were sin.

Jesus wished to make people kind, loving and considerate to each other. Many of his followers fought countless wars just to establish their dominance. Christianity, like all other religions, made many ethical rules about sex. Popes were always concerned about denouncing any form of adultery. They were hardly troubled with the obvious social evils, such as slavery, injustice and the exploitation of women.

On the contrary, priests were persistently anxious about illusions of witchcraft, vampires and other satanic activities. In fact, many powerful men in history never followed the teachings of the Buddha, Ram, Jesus or Muhammad but used their myths to attain power. Since time immemorial, men have been moulding gods in the ways that advance their own wishes.

10

Origin of Life

The planet earth is the most beautiful of all known celestial bodies. A variety of flora and fauna have painted it in many colours. Countless numbers of animals of diverse shapes and sizes thrive here. For ages, man, the most intelligent species on the earth, lived in a way similar to other animals. The entire intelligence, time and energy of man were engaged in fulfilling his basic needs of food, sex and shelter.

After the beginning of cultivation and domestication, priests began to notice animals closely. They observed that females gave birth. Now, they had another question: Who would have given birth to the first female? They spent hours discussing whether the hen or the egg came first. The priests of all the ancient civilizations pondered over the origin of life on the earth and made their own theories to explain it. Around four thousand years ago, priests wrote their theories in religious books.

For example, the ancient books of Mesopotamia mention that the sun made the sky and the earth, from the dead body of the devil. Finally, the sun created man to worship him (the sun). Ancient Egyptians believed that the sun rose from the depths of the ocean, created dry land and then created all creatures. Hindus, from antiquity till date, hold that Lord Brahma created life. Ancient Jews and Christians believed the theory of special creation, which is the most elaborate, interesting and widely accepted belief today. This theory was discussed in an earlier chapter on Judaism.

The origin of life on the earth has been an attractive topic of research for biologists as well. Aristotle, in 330 BCE, advocated that life originated spontaneously in different times from non-living organic matter. He believed that worms, wasps, mites and insects originated from rotting dung and mud. This belief continued well into the middle ages. In 1640 CE, Van Helmon claimed to have created a mouse in twenty-one days from his shirt. He marinated a sweat-soaked shirt in wheat flour and kept it in a dark room for those days.

Louis Pasteur (1862 CE) discarded the theory of spontaneous generation. To disprove this theory, he poured a nutritive soup in a glass flask with an airtight lid. He boiled it to kill all its living organisms and closed the lid. The soup in the closed flask remained unchanged and developed no putrefaction even after several days.

Later, he opened the lid and within a few days, the soup developed a foul smell. The bacteria of the air entered the soup through the lid and putrefied it. Pasteur concluded that life always takes birth from pre-existing life. The question of the origin of life, however, still remained unanswered.

Most of the religious theories about the origin of life were not logical, but people continued to posit faith in them for a long period. In 1850 CE, Charles Darwin discovered that living creatures did not come into being as they look today, but evolved from primitive life forms. He proposed that life originated with small and simple organisms such as blue-green algae, and these developed into bigger and complex ones. He explained how and why animals evolved from a simple form to a complex one. Later, palaeontology proved Darwin's theory. Today, all the religious theories have been discarded; they merely have historical importance.

Today, the biochemical origin of life called the Oparin–Haldane theory is widely accepted. This theory has been proven in the laboratory. Besides, scientists have enough palaeontological evidence to establish it. The theory hypothesizes that a small piece of the sun separated some four and a half billion years ago. This piece assumed the shape of a ball. In fact, it was separated from the sun just like a ball is made from a revolving wheel of a potter. That is the reason the ball began revolving around its axis and around the sun. This ball looked like a small sun and gave rise to the earth.

Initially, the temperature of the ball was as high as about 6000°C. This ball revolved around the sun, but the distance from its progenitor and the sub-zero temperatures in space allowed it to gradually cool down, over millions of years. The gases condensed into a molten core. Hydrogen and oxygen atoms combined to produce steam, which cooled and resulted in rain. It took around two hundred million years for the earth to cool down to 100°C.

Around four billion years ago, the heat of the earth was reduced enough to sustain the life. At this speed of cooling, the earth would have soon cooled to sub-zero temperatures of space. However, sunlight provided regular warmth to the earth. Thus, the sun managed to maintain a temperature necessary for the sustenance of life on the earth.

Around this time, the earth had a solid surface with a molten core. The pressure of the molten core often punctured the solid surface and gave rise to volcanoes. Elevations caused by volcanoes and the shifting of tectonic plates created mountains. Water filled the shallow areas creating the oceans. Oceanic water evaporated regularly and condensed to form clouds, causing rain. This led to the formation of various water streams and rivers. Rivers regularly changed their course that made the plains of river valleys.

Many elements like nitrogen remained gaseous even after cooling, thus forming a gaseous covering around the earth. The gaseous atmosphere had frequent occurrences of lightning, similar to the lightning seen during storms. The earth of that time had no ozone layer to protect it from the ultraviolet rays of the sun. Sunlight, lightning and ultraviolet rays initiated chemical reactions among the elements dissolved in oceanic water, which combined to form compounds.

The temperature of the surface of the earth further decreased, and the already formed compounds gave rise to hydrocarbons. These simple organic compounds gave rise to complex ones such as carbohydrates, fats and amino acids. These compounds are the basic constituents of every living body and are used as food as well. Thus, the oceanic water became a rich mixture of foods. J.B.S Haldane has described it as a 'hot dilute soup'.

Stanley Miller demonstrated the above process in a laboratory in 1953. He took a closed glass chamber and filled it with the basic elements of the earth. He provided a source of heat and light sparks in the chamber. Thus, he recreated the atmosphere that must have existed on the earth some four billion years ago. At the end of a week, he found that the elements had turned into a mixture of amino acids. Today, this experiment can be demonstrated even in high school laboratories.

In 1967 eminent scientist J. William Schoff detected twenty-two amino acids in a rock that was about four billion years old. Amino acids are the basic compounds of living beings. The recovery of those old amino acids provides concrete evidence of the chemical evolution of life.

Let's go back to the oceanic soup enriched with carbohydrates, fats and amino acids. These molecules united to form large colloidal masses. These colloidal masses were suspended in the hot diluted soup. The fat droplets in contact with these masses made a thin film around each mass. Soon, a chemical reaction started inside each colloidal mass and this was the early metabolism. These reactions had been going on at infinite places in the ocean for around a billion years. This infinite frequency of reactions gave rise to infinite chemical combinations.

Accidentally, the compounds of the oceanic soup made a special molecule called nucleic acid. Nucleic acid has a tendency to make its copy – the duplicating power. Colloidal masses along with nucleic acid made the earliest cells. The nucleic acid initiated making its copy and thus divided one cell into two – the process of reproduction.

Reproduction is the core technique of living cells that differentiates them from the non-living. The earliest cells were primitive and had no definite cellular structures. They could survive at high temperatures and humidity. Fossils of such earliest cells have been excavated in a rock that is about three and a half billion years old.

All these steps were spontaneous and happened at infinite numbers of spots in the ocean. In fact, each compound took millions of years to form. For example, the unicellular organism evolved from the hot dilute soup over a long period of half a billion years. The early bacterial cells might have consumed all the food in the hot dilute soup of the sea. Soon, these cells must have begun starving.

Fortunately, sunlight falling on the compounds of seawater made a chlorophyll-like compound. The chlorophyll molecule has a special property. This magical compound can combine water and carbon dioxide to make glucose with the help of sunlight. Thus, chlorophyll can store solar energy in glucose molecules. In fact, sunlight is the only source of energy on the earth.

The bacteria present around the compound could feed on glucose, and thus they survived. Bacteria made a complex with chlorophyll and gave rise to the blue-green algae around three billion years ago.

Scientists have excavated fossils of blue-green algae, around three billion years old, from Transvaal.

Formation of the chlorophyll-like compound in the hot dilute soup was a landmark in the process of origin of life. Every living being requires energy for its sustenance. The sun was there to shower its energy on the earth every day. Now the cells were capable of synthesizing food to fulfil their energy requirements.

Blue-green algae made food from sunlight, multiplied and ultimately engulfed the ocean. Besides, the chlorophyll in algae liberated breathable oxygen (O_2) as a waste product. Before the formation of chlorophyll, the atmosphere of the earth lacked breathable oxygen. Earlier, the atmosphere had only non-breathable oxygen – in its atomic state (O).

This release of oxygen by all the algae for over a billion years was another turning point. The earth's atmosphere was now filled with oxygen. The ultraviolet rays converted oxygen gas (O_2) into ozone gas (O_3). Ozone, being a lighter gas, collected at the periphery of the atmosphere.

This gas had the property of absorbing ultraviolet rays. Since the gas had almost enveloped the earth, it began protecting the earth from the deadly rays. Ozone protection gradually facilitated the development and survival of more complex life. The presence of oxygen facilitated a new efficient kind of food utilization.

The basic needs of animal life are oxygen, food and water. Although, after a long cooling period, water was available on the earth, there was no oxygen or food. The production of oxygen, ozone and food on the earth was facilitated by sunlight. As noted earlier, the sun kept the earth cosy enough to survive.

The process mentioned above looks a synchronized and planned reaction, as if someone was purposely making these complex compounds. The fact is that we are reading a story spanning two billion years in two minutes. These chemical reactions had been active at infinite numbers of places in the ocean for over a billion years. Since the reactions continued for such a long period and at multiple places, compounds like chlorophyll and nucleic acids were synthesized. Initially, these magical compounds might have been formed at a few places only. Once made, each molecule of the nucleic acid duplicated almost hourly for another billion years.

Blue-green algae took almost another billion years to evolve into complicated unicellular organisms. Fossils of such unicellular organisms have been found that date back to 1.85 billion years ago. At that time, there was no life on the dry surface of the earth. An aerial view of the earth would have revealed bare rocky mountains with green wavy oceans. The sun rose regularly; there was no one to worship it or hail it as god. Sunlight contained some ultraviolet rays, which endangered life. Eminent scientist Karl Sagan has suggested that during that time ozone layer was not thick enough; life could survive only in the ocean and that too at a depth of more than ten metres.

Unicellular organisms in seawater were either self-sufficient or parasites. The former had chlorophyll and could synthesize their food. Gradually, these gave rise to plants. Parasites had no chlorophyll. They survived on the food made by self-sufficient organisms and gave rise to the animal mode of life. All animals depended on plants for food directly or indirectly.

Gradually, both primitive organisms gave rise to more complex living beings. Scientists have fossil records of almost all species that developed from these two modes of life. Groups of unicellular organisms developed into simple multicellular organisms. These early organisms were simply a colony of various independent cells.

For example, fungus is a haphazard collection of cells; each cell can give rise to a new cell. These new ones remain attached to the parent cell. So they go on making a chain of cells. Each new cell may survive independently and can give rise to a new fungus colony. Scientists believe that most simple multicellular organisms such as fungus took birth around one billion years ago in the oceans.

These fungi evolved into jawless fishes. Simple algae evolved into the present complex algae. Fossils of fungi, complex algae, and jawless fishes have been excavated that date back 400 million years. They could be seen by the naked eye on the surface of the seawater; but there was still no inhabitation of land. Scientists believe that around 400 million years ago, the ozone layer became thick enough to shield the earth from harmful ultraviolet rays. This layer facilitated life on the surface of the oceanic water, and later on land.

Around 350 million years ago, small fern-like plants, wingless insects and frogs encroached coastal land for the first time. They had a complicated system of food and respiration. Frogs had by now developed male and female counterparts and so had sexual reproduction instead of the earlier asexual one. They gave rise to various lizards and other reptiles. Reptiles crawled out of the ocean and took possession of land around 280 million years ago. They spread the seeds of plants they had consumed in the sea, which gave rise to plants on land. The reptiles evolved into dinosaurs around 200 million years ago. Around 135 million years ago, larger plants with flowers beautified the earth. Dinosaurs, the largest creatures ever, became extinct around one hundred million years ago.

Around forty million years ago, primates like monkeys evolved. Over time, a few species of these monkeys evolved into great apes such as the chimpanzee. Only six million years ago, these great apes gave rise to bigger hominids. Around two million years ago, quadruped hominids in Africa began walking on two legs. Bipedal movement gave better visibility and mobility to them. These bipedal hominids Homo erectus gave rise to the modern man between 400 and 200 thousand years ago.

Fossil records of many species have established that various complex plants and animals evolved from simpler ones. The next important question is why every species evolved into a new, more complex and bigger species? Why did the fish evolve into the frog and the frog into the lizard? Biologists have enough evidence to explain the process. They have proved that only those organisms can survive who have an enormous power to reproduce or multiply.

This immense fertility leads to the explosion of population of each species, so much so that they suffer scarcity of food. For example, many insects produce millions of eggs each time. What would happen if each egg produces an insect and that survives to produce a million again and again? Soon, the entire earth would be covered with metres-thick layer of that insect.

In fact, newborn creatures, soon after birth, initiate a search for food. There is always limited food supply; and thus, there is a constant struggle for food among them. Only the strongest and the fittest of them survive the struggle to exist. Only the fittest survivors produce offspring.

Besides, survivors learn to adapt to the changing environmental conditions. Thus, they give birth to better offspring as their adaptations are carried genetically. In this way newer and newer species equipped with better survival instincts and qualities take birth. Again, this does not happen in one or two generations; even a small development takes thousands of generations.

For example, long ago, horses were only as big as the dogs of today; they evolved to the size of cows in millions of years. Cow-sized horses took another million of years to grow to the size of modern horses. Consider another example: big reptiles like crocodiles evolved into dinosaurs over a large span of eighty million years.

Coming to the evolution of man: The human race came into being between 400 and 200 thousand years ago. Excavated human skulls of those times have a brain as big as that of a modern man. However, their intelligence (IQ) was much lower as compared to today's standards. It is evident from the fact that they had not yet developed language, morals, clothing, farming and other features of developed intelligence. Today, the size of the brain of a man is the same, but their IQ has increased. How could intelligence grow without a change in size and structure of the brain?

Scientists have discovered the cause behind the breeding behaviour of man. Biologists have extensively studied the breeding pattern of different apes and compared it with that of the human being. Females of chimps and gorillas mate only during the mating season at ovulation. However, females of the ape gibbon have no such mating season and can mate on almost any day of the year.

This difference in sexual behaviour of these two kinds of apes differentiated their modes of lifestyle. Chimps and gorillas live in groups dominated by one male, accompanied by many females and their children. A gibbon lives in a single monogamous family that comprises one couple and their children.

Men inherited a sexual life with an almost continuous mating desire like gibbons. Therefore, at some stage of evolution, men must have adopted the family structure similar to that of gibbons. Regular libido of males facilitated family life and caring of females during late pregnancy and childbirth.

Consequently, females preferred to mate with males they found to be most caring. This primitive kind of living together gave rise to the selection of life partners. The regular mating desire of males also facilitated the selection of partner. Animals which require mating just once a year do not bother to select their partner.

Not only selection of partners, men made some primitive rules regarding breeding. Among all animals, a brother-sister or a ward-parent duo might mate to produce offspring, which is called incestuous behaviour. At one point in time, almost all independent clusters of men on the earth enforced an incest taboo. Why and when did men begin banning incest?

Anthropologists believe that the incest taboo began to evolve during prehistoric time. They suggest three theories to explain the reasons behind this radical change of behaviour. The childhood familiarity theory suggests that siblings and parent – who lived together from childhood – are not attracted sexually to each other.

The family disruption theory propounds that incestuous behaviour initiated a kind of sexual competition among the family members. Many times this leads to rivalry and quarrels especially in large families. The unity of the family was a must to protect it from wild animals and to carry out large hunts. In fact, when two or more males fought for the same female in the family, the elders made a rule to restrain all males, and thus keep the family united.

The inbreeding theory propounds that early men must have had a belief that incest produces an abnormal child. The theory has been proved scientifically today. A study has revealed that about 40 per cent of incestuously produced children were abnormal. In contrast, spouses not related to each other by family lineage gave birth to less than 1 per cent abnormal offspring.

Early men must have learnt this fact by experience. Developing language and memory were the main reasons behind this learning. Today also, incest is a serious taboo in almost every society; although its extent differs in each.

Selection of the partner and prohibition of incest were learnt behaviours, but some unintentional factors also influenced breeding. Various climatic vicissitudes caused forced migration of men and encouraged mating between distant tribes. For example, the last Ice Age locked so much water in the north and south poles that the sea level fell by nearly a hundred metres.

Islands like Britain and Japan joined the main lands. Australia and Asia joined together so that the Asiatic animals could go all the way to Australia and meet the kangaroo. During the Ice Age, people had to move out of the frozen north. These periods of mass movements resulted in mating between the migrating human bands.

Biologists have discovered that better progeny could be achieved through the mating of two individuals of different lineage. The factors mentioned above encouraged mating between the best partners both by chance and by choice. Man achieved wiser progeny after many generations by selecting his mating partners. Genetic modification was the main factor behind the manifold growth of human intelligence without change in the size and structure of his brain.

Thus, the human race practised a breeding pattern that facilitated production of wiser generations. Gradually, after thousands of generations, the modern wise man was born.

From these facts, it becomes obvious that life was not created by some power intentionally. In fact, it was a theological blunder to declare that God is the creator of all plants and animals. Just observe how all animals remain busy all through the day, killing one another. Each animal has to eat one or the other plant or animal. Would a merciful creator consciously create such violent animals?

Plants are supposed to be primitive and less developed than animals, but the possession of chlorophyll makes them self-sufficient. This magical compound is found in all green plants. This enables them to manufacture their own food and they never need to kill anyone for their survival.

Had God really designed animals, He would have made them non-violent as well. Of course, God could have easily made a peaceful world just by gifting chlorophyll to animals as well.

Alas! If mankind had chlorophyll in their skin, it would never have required to study, work, labour or make any effort for food. Men would have to take a daily sunbath to satiate their hunger. In that situation, the world would have had no poverty, crime, inequality, exploitation or slavery. Just by having chlorophyll in the skin, mankind could have escaped its entire barbaric history. On the obverse side, with chlorophyll in our skin, we would not have made any scientific progress either.

11

Why Gods Are Still Alive

After a study of the previous chapters, it is obvious that during the last five thousand years, mankind created many gods. People wasted time and money to please their gods. They believed that the flattered gods would bless them, but their gods did nothing for them. On the contrary, people tolerated many social evils and diseases due to the fear of gods. These people were mentally enslaved by their priests. Ancient people committed these mistakes out of ignorance; they lived in darkness.

Today, the light of science is all around us. By virtue of science, modern people are no longer scared of the unseen. The entire universe is not a mystery today. Mankind has found remedies for all the previous miseries of epidemic diseases and famines. Thus, modern men rarely face mystery, misery and helplessness. Therefore, the concept of divine powers has lost its relevance. Our ancestors had enough reasons to imagine and worship many divine powers, but the present generation has none.

Today, literacy of the masses all over the world has increased. Modern people are curious about each new scientific discovery. They wish to explore new happenings on the globe through news channels. On the contrary, the knowledge of the modern educated masses about religions comprises age-old convictions only.

Today, the burning question is why people are not interested to know about the gods they worship daily. There are many who worship their gods for an hour daily. If they devote this hour in reading the history of gods, they may not need to worship any god after a few months.

Schools often teach national history to the new generation. But the religious history of the nation is not yet taught. At the same time, people are not inquisitive about the history of religions. Today, only the history of religions and gods can enlighten the people about the truth.

Just a few decades ago, only books and newspapers held knowledge. These methods had their own limitations. For example, one could have wasted his life to read the books of one religion only. Today, the Internet has opened new avenues for the acquisition of knowledge. Almost all ancient religious books are available on the Internet in popular languages. Besides this, a few encyclopedias provide a wide knowledge about religions. Surprisingly, modern men use the Internet to acquire most of their knowledge, but for the knowledge of religion they rely on priests.

Today, one of the most perplexing subjects is persistence of the god delusion. Why do people still believe in a fabricated concept even after enough advancements in science? Why are gods still alive despite the fact that science has disproved their existence? Today, people believe in many scientific inventions but they ignore the scientific opinions about gods. Almost all devotees have discarded the major section of their religious books that described remedies for diseases. On the contrary, they still worship those books.

For example, today Hindus have discarded a major section of the Vedas that describes magic and sacrifices to cure diseases. Modern Hindu priests do not chant hymns to heal patients. Instead, they follow modern medicine. At the same time, Hindus continue to chant flattering hymns for gods from the same books. Similarly, Christians and Jews do not follow remedies mentioned in the Bible, but they still worship the Bible. Today, devotees of almost all religions believe in modern medicine but continue to revere their perceived gods.

There must be some concrete reasons behind this fallacy in this scientific era. There are four pillars of the religions of today: the theory of sins, illiteracy and poverty, ancient literature and modern priests. Without these pillars, each religion cannot sustain itself. The increasing ambitions of men, coupled with their expectations of miracles and the limitations of science, have also helped to sustain the concept of God. People also need a benevolent protector who apparently fulfil their interests. People require some saviour-or patron-like protective figure that may be an imaginative one. Without this support, life seems difficult. Many people get depressed without the support of some almighty power. The human desire for solace and comfort has led to the persistence of the most cherished illusion of mankind. It is necessary to explore how these factors have contributed to sustain the delusion of gods.

Theory of Sins – the Violation of God-made Rules

Today, the theory of sins and good deeds provides a strong foundation to religions. Most sacred laws are upheld due to the sanctity of such a theory. The holy grail in quest for absolution is to be found in the codices of almost all religions. The true allure of religion lies in its promise of forgiveness. The sinner will be saved, if only he follows the true path of the lord, the true path being the sole proprietorship of the religion. This theory is the soul of all religions. Without this soul religions are like dead bodies.

Almost all religions had propagated more or less similar convictions about sins – the violation of God-made rules. When and why did the theory develop? Did some god himself descend from the heavens to imbue man with an acute sense of ethics and morals? Why did sins invite the scourge of gods, and why did the benevolent acts of humanity please him? What were the events that led to the establishment of this theory?

This theory is already discussed in Chapter 6. Before the invention of agriculture, nomadic men faced hunger, wild animals and adverse weather. But the advent of farming and socialization, led to epidemic diseases, famines, poverty, exploitation, injustice and crimes. The disparity in the distribution of incomes gave birth to social classes. Poverty led to poor hygiene, lack of adequate shelter and food which in turn paved the way for diseases and deaths. Consequently, the suffering individuals began to question their gods.

Priests had maintained that God was a philanthropic entity and the well-being of his subjects was his primary concern. However, the human suffering raised many questions. If some almighty and kind power had deliberately made the living being, why did he also make the evils? To establish the concept of a kind but almighty divine power, it became mandatory for priests to discover the cause of the human evils.

The dilemma of evil had always been a nightmare for the architects of religions. Draftsmen of all religions fabricated their own explanation of human miseries. In their multiple capacities as the caretakers of society, priests were concerned with the rising crime rates as well.

To maintain law and order, priests and kings made social rules themselves and declared them to be the divine word. They proclaimed that the non-observance of the rules – the sins – provoked divine anger. Gods punished the sinners through various human miseries.

The concept began around four thousand years ago; King Hammurabi made the first moral rules in Mesopotamia. The rules were engraved on a flat stone. At the top of the inscription, the king was depicted receiving the rules from the sun. Similarly, priests and kings all over the world made moral rules and declared that following their rules was the pious duty of every citizen.

Later, Moses came up with a refined version of the theory. He declared that God had ordered every citizen to follow the Ten Commandments – the moral rules. Besides, Moses warned the people that God Yahweh would punish the violators through plague.

Besides Moses, other prophets also propagated that all human miseries were god's punishment for sins. Similarly, human happiness was god's reward for good moral behaviour. Thus, many religions, despite being largely independent in origin, developed similar theories of divine punishment and reward. These served to maintain the observance of a moral code. During the ancient and medieval times, this theory was a good method to enforce the social rules.

Soon, the theory of sin attracted many sceptic philosophers. Through their simple logic, they pinpointed many loopholes in the theory. Not only the philosophers, but common people as well began complaining that there were many sinners who lived comfortable lives without being punished. On the other hand, many saints who followed all the morals suffered from diseases. After facing these practical problems, contemporary priests began to search for an explanation.

This puzzle was solved by a great person who himself was not a priest. His conjecture has not been proved or disproved till date. He propagated that good people suffered due to the sins of their previous births. The present-day sinners would be punished in their next birth. He declared that all human suffering like diseases, inequality and exploitation was the result of sins committed in the previous births.

This theory found great popularity and therefore continued for more than two millennia. Let us consider why the propaganda of this theory has not been exposed yet. In fact, there is no way to determine whether an individual has led more than one life. Even if rebirths were to be granted legitimacy for the sake of argument, the sins of one's past life cannot be known.

This theory was propagated by the Buddha in India. He asserted that human birth was sorrow, age was sorrow, death was sorrow, disease was sorrow, etc. He advised non-violence and asked his followers to lead a morally upright life to escape sorrow. The famous enlightenment of the Buddha was not a miraculous meeting with God: it was an invention that sufferings of human race were the result of the sins of their previous births.

The doctrine of the Buddha comprised a theory of sins and their consequences in the next birth. The Buddha taught that following a morally fulfilling life would lead to a happy, prosperous and healthy rebirth. His philosophy did not require its followers to worship any god. The theory was a great logic almost impossible to disapprove and, therefore, attracted a large number of devotees.

The Buddha's theory took a few centuries to spread. However, a millennia later, half the world's population was Buddhist. Many religions also adopted this theory to explain the sufferings afflicting its followers. A case in point is its incorporation into Hinduism. Many historians believe that Jesus was also influenced by the Buddha. Christians believe that everyone will account for his sins on the Day of Judgement. Thus, this theory was believed by a majority of the world's population.

Gradually, punishment for the sins of previous births came to be accepted as a scientific theory to explain suffering. Without this, the concept of kind gods might have been discarded after the painful death of a famous saint by disease. Many famous saints died a painful and premature death. The concept of the human soul and its rebirth acted as the core of the sinning theory, and has kept it alive till date.

Why do gods wait for the next birth to convict his self-created puppets (men)? Are gods not capable of punishing them in their present birth? Ideally, their acts must be followed by divine punishments or rewards immediately. Practically, this does not happen. It is said: 'Justice delayed is justice denied.'

Around 2,400 years ago, Greek philosopher Epicurus declared that the presence of evil in the world denied God's existence. He said: 'Is He (God) willing to prevent evil, but is not able to? Then He is impotent. Is He able to prevent evil, but is not willing to? Then He is malevolent. Is He both able and willing? Then where did the evil come from? Is he neither able nor willing? Then why call him God?'

Had gods punished the sinners in their present birth, it would have been justified. Not only would it ensure justice, it would have eliminated all crimes on the earth and removed the necessity of policemen and guns. Punishment for the sins committed in the present life is conceivable; but its postponement to next birth casts doubts over its credibility. Even today, many people are convinced that this theory of sins is true.

The fallacious nature of this theory can be easily shown. Hindus are taught that each animal suffers punishment for sins committed during its seven previous births. Therefore, the Hindu almighty God has to closely monitor each animal during all its seven births. God has to watch each animal individually throughout its lifetime to determine the bent of its deeds.

Let us take an hour as the standard unit of crime (that means it takes at least one hour to commit a crime). Thus, God would need to record each hour in an individual's lifespan. Fifty years ago, God would have relied upon eyewitnesses and must have maintained a written record.

Let's imagine how God may keep his records today. In the twenty-first century, his record keeping would include videography. To record the activities of each person, one video camera would follow him regularly. Video films of three hours require about one gigabyte (GB) of computer space. Activity of one day of each person would take 8 GB space to record. Therefore, the sum of the video footage of seven lifetimes would require 8 × 365 (no of days in a year) × 60 (years of average life) × 7 (births) GB of space. This figure exceeds a million. Thus, a million GB of space is needed to store the life of an individual.

The hard disc of a common computer stores around 500 GB. Therefore, for each soul God would maintain a huge computer with 2,000 disks. God would maintain one office to keep one such computer. God's compound would need one billion such offices for Hindus only. It is funny that God, who has not yet provided houses to a billion Indians, has maintained as many offices to punish them.

What about the other animals? Collecting data for all of them is nearly impossible. Still, it can be presumed that the almighty God would manage. He could reduce the cost and workload by group video photography of the smaller animals such as ants and fleas.

God would face another difficulty while keeping the record of unseen bacteria and viruses. Firstly, they are infinite in number: one drop of water may contain millions. Secondly, he would require microscopic videography to tape them. However, God can forgive them, since these bacteria and viruses help him to punish the non-believers and sinners by causing diseases! Today, it is almost impossible to watch and memorize the activity of each and every creature on the earth. However, monitoring and recording human deeds is now possible with the coming of technology.

Alas! The monitoring of human activities is not enough for justice! Just by storing the data, God cannot do justice. For justice, the sinners must be punished, and saints must be rewarded. God would face a real challenge in law enforcement. God has to appoint many jurors to watch the recorded videos. One officer would take around 420 years (expected life [60 years] × 7 births) to watch the videos of seven births of one soul. To get the same work done quickly, say in one year, God would require 420 such officers.

Today, if God wished to punish someone in one year, he would require 420 officers for that person only. Thus, to punish the whole population, God would need a huge staff – around 420 times the number of people alive. Hindu religious books mention that God has appointed only one officer named Chitragupta for this job. The calculations mentioned above indicate that Chitragupta alone is not enough!

God would also have to ensure the honesty of his executives. How would he create such a large number of honest, justice-loving, and truthful staff? If God made his officers from the same soil he created the first male and female, these officers would also begin sinning. God would have to monitor his officers as well! Apart from monitoring his staff, God would require many planets to ensure their food and shelter. The punishment of man seems to be God's punishment as well.

Not only Hindus, Christians also believe they would suffer the punishment of their sins on the Day of Judgement. They are curious to know when that day would come. By the above calculation, they can conclude that the delay is due to Peter's inadequacy. As long as Peter alone is doing the job, they can live the life of their choice without the fear of punishment after death!

The theory of sins can be disapproved by a simple logic. Religious theologies have propagated that each human has a physical body and a soul inside. Only the physical body commits the sins, not the soul. The soul is considered pure and an extension of the supreme God. Whenever a living being dies, its body decomposes and mixes into the soil. Immediately after death, its soul becomes free. After some time the soul takes birth in the shape of a second body.

Normally, God punishes the second body. Obviously, the second body is being punished for the sins committed by the first body. To punish the second body for the sins committed by the first body is sheer injustice. Thus, punishment of sins in the same lifetime is just. Punishment in the next birth is fabricated and unjust concept.

In fact, the theory of sins had two basic purposes: to frighten the masses and to establish the kindness of God, despite the human sufferings. There is no relevance of this theory for God as well. Why should God be concerned about the acts and behaviour of his created animals? They may be dancing, drinking or dating.

This can be explained by comparing the creation of God with the creation of a car-manufacturing company. For example, Ford made millions of vehicles in the last 100 years. Similarly, God made billions of men. Furthermore, the company produced all its cars, whereas God created only the first man and woman. Thus, Ford has been doing a bigger job than God for its product.

Imagine what would happen if Mr Ford – the creator of the cars – begins to expect some worship similar to God! Each car owner would be obliged to mount an image of Ford above the rear-view mirror. Then, each car would be sold only after a written contract with the purchaser stating that its driver would follow a strict protocol before ignition each morning. The driver would also have to ignite an incense stick and sing a flattering song with folded hands invoking Mr Ford. The song may run like this:

> Creator and nurturer of this car,
> Mr Ford, you are great!
> All the adjectives in dictionaries are not enough
> for you, the great!
> I am starting your car as per protocol,
> for blessings and for escaping from your rage!
> Long live Ford...

Apart from offering such prayers, riders have to follow strict dietary rules as per the choice of Ford. Boozing and obscenity in the car would attract punishment. Besides, the owner would not be allowed to use the car for transporting disgusting materials. For execution of the above rules, the company would have to depute officers to ensure that the driver is behaving as per the contract. Ford would have to ascertain punishment for non-followers such as withdrawal of after-sale service.

If the employees of the company remained occupied with these arrogant ambitions of their owner, they would have no time for making new cars. In fact, each good company is only concerned over the defects in the latest model of their cars, as their defects have to be rectified in the subsequent model. Therefore, in the last 100 years, the car technology has improved many times.

Similarly, God must be concerned only about the manufacturing defects of his product, the children. He must try to rectify the defects in each newborn. In fact, human diseases are the major manufacturing defects in the products of God. Mankind suffered from the worst kinds of epidemic diseases for three millennia after the beginning of agriculture. After wrestling with the problem for a long time, just fifty years ago, mankind discovered remedies for some of these diseases.

But today, mankind is facing new diseases such as malignancies, AIDS, diabetes, hypertension, psychosis and vascular diseases. Prevalence of all these diseases has increased tenfold in the last decades. Just fifty years ago, one woman out of a hundred suffered from carcinoma of the breast; today it kills one in nine. Deteriorating physical and mental health of mankind indicates that if God is its creator, he is least concerned with the defects in the products of his factory.

Thus, the presence of evil in the world proves that if God exists, he is either not omnipotent or he is not kind. Sufferings endured by the best of God's creations disprove his existence. Through the logic mentioned above it appears that each sufferer would quit worship. However, ironically most humans, after an episode of suffering, become more God-fearing.

For example, today, many patients suffering from serious diseases waste their time and money on rituals and miracles. Many businessmen visit famous temples and donate liberally after each big loss. Many couples are seen performing various rituals to obtain Gods' blessings to beget a son. Many lovers are seen visiting temples frequently to woo their beloved.

Most of the frequent visitors to temples are miserable people. Rather than work to improve their conditions, miserable people rely on worship and devotion. It is rare to find a believer who turned sceptic after facing a misery. Failures of the past, miseries of the present and fears of the future are still twisting the arm of mankind to believe and worship gods.

In fact, after facing suffering, men commonly blame gods and not themselves. Soon, they resort to worship, donation and ritual. Why do even educated people suppose that some god or the other is responsible for each misery? This conviction has two benefits. Firstly, it makes someone else accountable for their follies. Most of the time, people themselves are responsible for their misery. Today, most of the human miseries are the result of poor skills, lack of effort or behaviour. But people refuse to be held accountable.

For example, ego is one of the major causes of human suffering today. Many people have spoiled their lives just to satisfy their ego. Egoistic people are usually staunch believers of gods. After each failure, only gods can keep their ego intact. They always believe that their suffering is punishment for their sins committed in the previous birth. This way they escape accountability for their actions. Besides, accepting their mistakes hurts their ego.

Secondly, after blaming the gods, people begin to worship them.

It gives them the illusion that soon, they will be happy. These two factors are two edges of the same sword that causes more harm than help. Since people do not identify their shortcomings, they usually repeat their mistakes. Besides, this reliance on gods makes people complacent. Thus, despite the advancement of science, the advent of new diseases and problems has managed to sustain man's belief in gods. Gods will continue to exist, as long as mankind continues to suffer.

Illiteracy and Poverty

The root causes of a majority of today's problems are illiteracy and poverty. Poverty is the scourge of humanity. Today's poverty is no longer limited to a deficiency of food and shelter, but also extends to inequality. Gods, poverty and illiteracy seem to be intricately linked.

For example, almost no religious scripture encouraged its followers to become educated and rich. Authors of the Bible wrote: 'Blessed are the poor for they shall inherit the kingdom of God. It is extremely difficult for a rich person to enter heaven.' Besides, the popes propagated the Bible as the sole source of knowledge and placed an effective ban on scientific books.

Any person, who propounded any concept contrary to the Bible, was considered an atheist and he was punished like a criminal. For example, the Bible mentions that the sun revolves around the earth. It is now common knowledge that the earth revolves around the sun. All those who held the latter faith like Galileo were forced to recant, by threat of force or excommunication. This lie was enforced by the Church for many generations. However, the discovery of the truth left a big dent on the credibility of the Bible and its God.

The Buddha advised begging as the most pious way of life. This encouraged poverty. Ancient Hindu books mentioned that poverty was an outcome of sins committed in seven previous births, so the poor should accept it as their destiny. The Hindu poet Maluka wrote: 'Snakes do no job, birds do no work; it is the god Ram who blesses food to everyone.' This rhyme propagates that no effort should be made to procure one's food, since god Ram provides food for his devotees. All these teachings ultimately encouraged poverty.

Today, the root cause behind poverty is overpopulation. No religious literature advocated population control. Rather, religious books advocated producing more children. Even today, most illiterates believe that children are the gifts of gods; so they try their best to beget as many as possible.

Due to this conviction, the population of illiterate people has increased in the last fifty years. Today, only illiterate couples have six or more children, and as a consequence they cannot afford to properly bring them up. Under the guise of atonement, poor people have lived in inhuman conditions for ages, and the possibility of their emancipation is precluded by their belief in this form of penance.

Furthermore, society introduced casteism and slavery to exploit the weak. Again, people enforced these inhuman practices through the fear of gods. For three millennia, people tolerated such atrocities because they believed that casteism and slavery were punishments inflicted by gods.

It is surprising that priests did not oppose these practices. Rather, they were more concerned about the sexual relations of the masses. Many priests punished adulterers and prostitutes. They punished the people marrying out of their religion, but never cared to take action against criminals. Priests of almost all religions remained silent about inequality, slavery, casteism and exploitation. These were major social issues that exist even today. Instead of opposing social wrong, priests – the architects of religions – supported these man-made evils.

The great philosopher Karl Marx rightly said that religion was the opium of the masses as it could make their sufferings bearable. He further added that religion could give only illusory happiness. The thought that Lord Almighty is taking care of all creatures can help the poor psychologically. But it actually makes them complacent and reduces their desire to make a conscientious effort to solve their own problems.

Priests promised and reassured the poor that if they behaved righteously and worshipped gods, they would be blessed. Thus, priests continued this illogical system to retain their dominance of society. Priests did nothing to cure disease of poverty, but prescribed palliatives to their followers – the promise of a better tomorrow. In this regard, Charles Kinsley, a canon of the Church of England, wrote: 'We have used the Bible as a book to keep the poor in order.'

Karl Marx was probably the first to foresee and expose religion as a tool of the ruling classes to exploit the weak. He believed that the fear of God helped the mighty and prevented the rebellion of the oppressed.

Class and caste exploitation can be understood through an example. During ancient times, Indian society was divided into four major castes. Hindu scriptures propagated that the caste system was made by the gods. The people of lower caste suffered the punishments of the sins of previous births. Therefore, the lower-caste people rarely revolted against the inhuman treatment meted out to them.

Dr Bhim Rao Ambedkar and other leaders made marathon efforts to abolish this system. During that period, the masses had complete faith in their religious books. Therefore, initially Ambedkar criticized Hindu gods to reduce the fear of gods from the minds of the lower castes. He advised them to join Buddhism, a religion without a god or a caste system. Buddhism considered all people equal. Ambedkar modified the religious convictions of lower-caste people. Only after this, he could manage to motivate the lower castes to ask for equal rights.

Today, many well-informed and prosperous people around the globe have pushed their religion and gods into oblivion. They worship regularly, but do not allow the interference of religion in their ways of career, prosperity, romance, etc. They frequently tweak the ancient rules of their religion to fulfil their desires. At the same time, a large number of people still follow their religion word by word. These are the people who are usually fooled by modern priests.

As discussed earlier, each subsequent misfortune enforces their faith in gods. They believe that gods will bless them with all the amenities that others are enjoying. Therefore, they do not work hard for the betterment of their life. Illiteracy and poverty can be put to an end within one generation. Just give birth to a single child and work hard to educate him/her without expecting any help from any divine source. Persistent struggle is the only solution to our miseries, not some miraculous intervention of gods.

Ancient Divine Literature

For ages, the masses have been receiving the knowledge of gods by word of mouth. Parents tell the stories of their gods to their children. Parents were also informed by their parents and priests orally. Priests learnt the stories of gods from their parents. What was the origin of this divine knowledge? In fact, all these were mentioned in ancient books. All the gods and the religions of today were introduced through ancient writings. Let's consider the origin of these books again.

As studied earlier, farmers worldwide suffered from new miseries such as diseases, poverty, inequality, exploitation and crimes. A few prophets or philosophers began a quest for discovering the cause and remedy of human sufferings. They introduced morals, magic, worship or rituals to relieve the suffering masses. By the time of the prophets, priests had learnt to write. Many priests wrote down the divine remedies and moral teachings of the prophets. Those ancient writings fashioned the organized religions of today.

Learning to write was a great invention, but it gave rise to one big problem. The myths written in these holy books were treated as actual events by subsequent generations. In fact, several ancient writings narrated the magic performed by contemporary prophets. These were either fiction or poetic exaggeration of the actual events. These were written decades after the deaths of the prophets which made them difficult to verify. Gradually, the masses considered these magical stories as real events or the history.

For example, Abraham, Moses or Jesus never claimed that they had divine powers during their lifetimes. Neither did they perform their magic publicly. Even if they wished they could not do so! How could Moses exhibit a live demonstration of transforming a stick into a snake? Centuries later, authors of the Bible wrote that Moses exhibited the snake magic in the court of the Egyptian king. Not only Moses, the magician of the king also played the same trick.

Similarly, Jesus himself never propagated that he could do magic. Authors of the Bible mention that Jesus performed many magic tricks. Historians believe that Jesus was not capable of performing the magic mentioned in the Bible. For example, Jesus revived a dead person. How could Jesus claim to revive a dead person? Had it been true all the dead bodies of the town would have stacked up at his door.

If Jesus could bestow life, he would have lived till today! Christians believed that Jesus took birth to alleviate the sufferings of the human race. Had Jesus survived, mankind would not have faced the diseases, exploitations, injustices and wars it had suffered from during the last 2,000 years.

Similarly, the Bible mentions that Jesus was crucified to death. He was buried, and on third day he returned to life again – the Resurrection. Revival of Jesus was the most important magical event that established him as the Son of God. Today, the only evidence of this magic is the Bible. The book mentions that three days after his death, three ladies of the city found his sepulchre empty. Why did they open it? Was it a routine in Jerusalem to open each grave after a few days?

Besides, the Bible mentions that three days after the death of Jesus, devotees saw him alive at a few places in Jerusalem. Had it been true, the devotees would have chased him. Jesus addressed a public meeting before he was crucified. Surprisingly, he addressed no meeting after his revival. He would have received a red-carpet welcome.

According to the Bible, it appears that after the Resurrection, Jesus was hiding somewhere in Jerusalem. Why did Jesus hide himself after his revival? Jesus was probably frightened that the Jews would kill him again! Present-day historians believe that either the corpse of Jesus was stolen or he was injured badly by crucifixion, but did not die.

In fact, Jesus was not considered the Son of God during his lifetime. Many years after the death of Jesus, his stories were written in the Bible. The authors glorified him through poetic exaggerations. Once the magical stories of Jesus were documented in the Bible, the readers considered these as true happenings. Later generations had no way to disapprove these stories. Thus, Jesus was designated as the Son of God only after his magical acts were documented in the Bible.

Similarly, the Buddha was not identified as a god in his lifetime by his disciples or any of the Hindu priests. He was recognized as a great teacher. He himself denied the existence of gods. He never recognized any Hindu gods such as Vishnu, Shiva or Shakti. Neither had he exhibited any magic in his large teaching spell of almost half a century.

Five hundred years after his death, the Hindu religious books introduced him as an incarnation of god Vishnu. Besides, many

Buddhist books also portrayed him as a god. These books wrote many magical stories about him. Only then people started to worship his idol. It is obvious that the people followed the books.

Let's consider another classic example of one of the Hindu gods. Poet Valmiki wrote the Ramayana and portrayed its hero Ram as a great king and human being. Even after the Ramayana, Hindus did not recognize Ram as a god for a long period, since Valmiki did not glorify Ram as a god. After 2,000 years, Tulsidas wrote the story again. He glorified the hero Ram as an incarnation of god Vishnu. The new story was written only 400 years ago; after which Hindus began recognizing Ram as a god.

After the new story, people began to worship Ram, Sita and Hanuman. It is evident from the fact that history rarely mention worship of Ram before Tulsidas. Besides, almost all the temples of Ram were built after the new story was written. The stories of the Bible, the Puranas, and other religious books were written almost 2,000 years ago. The problem is that people consider these to be legitimate history as there was no alternative.

These ancient books were written on plant leaves or bark such as papyrus. Priests had to prepare new copies of the original texts frequently because of the deterioration of the writing material. Without any strict publishing rules, the new editions contained many of the beliefs and prejudices of its preservers. Apart from these, people adapted new languages and alphabets with time. Consequently, priests translated the books in popular languages. After much copying and translation, priests altogether changed the text of the ancient books.

For example, the Bible was first written around 2,000 years ago, and priests copied it frequently. The printing press was invented by Gutenberg only a few centuries ago. Before Gutenberg, the Bible of today must have been copied manually hundreds of times. Each copying provided an opportunity to modify the text.

Furthermore, the Bible was initially written in Greek and was translated into English only after several centuries. These translations and copying gave rise to many versions of the Bible in the late middle ages. To resolve this confusion, King James's version written in 1611 CE was designated as the authorized version of the Bible. Thus, the modern Bible cannot be considered an exact replica of the original version.

Let us consider another example. The Rig Veda was first written around 3,500 years ago. The oldest surviving manuscript of the Rig Veda was written only 400 years ago. These were handwritten on bark of birch. There is a long period of 3,000 years between the first transcription of the Rig Veda and its oldest manuscript available today. During that period, the Rig Veda must have been manually copied thousands of times. Each copying provided opportunity to interpolate and modify the Rig Veda.

In fact, these ancient books are like old rocks. They provide an insight into the lives of the people living in those times. The authors of these books had different problems and solutions. Ancient priests wrote the stories to give moral lessons to the masses from that time until today. These stories continues to guide the masses from that time until today. However, the real tragedy is that these ancient scriptures are still considered by devotees to be an accurate history of the era. Had the books on Harry Potter been written 2,000 years ago, a large population of the world today would have been worshipping Harry.

There is another problem with ancient books. Other than the Bible, all ancient books are still read in obsolete languages. In fact, priests propagated that the worshippers could obtain God's blessings only if they chanted the holy books in their original languages. Therefore, most devotees read the books in their original languages. They have read or listened their holy book many times in their life, but never understood its meaning.

Not only common man, many modern priests also fail to understand the meaning of the holy books they chant daily. Today, only a handful of scholars can decipher the meaning of these books. A few of them have translated these into the languages of the masses. By and large, the translated versions are authentic and any serious reader can interpret the motive of the original authors.

The educated generation of today is wiser than the great philosophers of the past such as Aristotle or Plato. How could they believe that God had sent ten plagues? How could they agree that sperm from the right testicle gave birth to a male child? They would laugh over the idea that human diseases were caused by the wrath of demons and gods. Modern people could not exhume graves to treat the patients of tuberculosis. They could not sacrifice animals during epidemics.

Although, modern people worship as per the procedure laid down in the ancient books, they do not follow the remedies mentioned in these books – the magic, the incantations or the sacrifices. They never think of going to a temple for treatment. If the teachings of the ancient books are followed today, the world would require neither doctors nor hospitals, only an abundance of priests and temples.

For example, the ancient Hindu priests chanted hymns to treat their patients. The Atharva Veda mentions hundreds of charms or hymns to treat all the ailments under the sun. The book advises one short poem or hymn to be recited in front of patients suffering from a particular disease. There are different poems for each common illness like fever and even for specific problems like sterility. There are poems to become invisible and produce a male child. For example, the following is a hymn to find a husband for a young girl:

> Agni, may this girl find a husband.
> Then verily King Soma makes her happy.

> Agni, may her lover come, to please us.
> Seeking this maid and bringing us good fortune.
> May she be soon made happy with a husband.
> To be blessed by Soma and God,
> I recite this bridal oracle.

Today, the hymns of the Atharva Veda are not recited to cure illness. But, priests are still reciting hymns to beget a male child or a husband for the girls. They recite these hymns in the ancient language of the scripture, so the devotees cannot understand their meaning.

In fact, after reading the translation of ancient books, today's educated people can easily find out the truth. Everyone can easily perceive the superstitions these books propagate. The Rig Veda or the Bible seems divine due to the barriers presented by language. Surprisingly, modern people are not curious to read even the books of their own religions. They simply believe the lies fabricated by priests.

For example, most of these books narrate that one kind God created men and other creatures. They also stated that God hated any kind of violence. Today, it is obvious that all animals have to kill other animals or plant to satiate their hunger. It is surprising that the merciful God consciously created all these hungry and murderous animals. Why would anyone destine his creations to be killed and eaten up by another of his creations? If some almighty God intentionally created animals, he could easily have fashioned non-violent animals similar to plants.

Furthermore, many religious books reveal that mankind is the best creation of God. Had God created men, there would have been no disparity amongst his various creations. Normally, parents provide equal education, opportunities, wealth, etc., to all their children. Why did not God, being the supreme parent of mankind, distribute health, wealth, beauty, etc., equally amongst his children?

Why are only some people healthy, while others are sick? Why are only a few people rich and the vast majority poor? Why are only a few people happy? Why do many people suffer an early death? There are people who cannot earn their own bread. In contrast, there are those who have collected resources enough for millions. How can one conceive that the same God made both Bill Gates and the poor masses living miserably in slums?

Human suffering challenges the very existence of a creator. Had there been a kind, just and loving power to create and govern mankind, there would have been no place for inequality, exploitation, disease and injustice in the world. Surprisingly, mankind faced and still continues to face a number of miseries. Nevertheless, they still believe their gods to be almighty, kind and helpful.

Modern men waste time worshipping gods; they do not even bother to read their religious books. Today, most of the devotees have not read the book of their religion in the language known to them. In fact, science could develop only after scientists refuted the teachings of these ancient books. It is evident from the fact that in the last century, mankind invented more than what it did over many millennia. Thus, ancient scriptures deferred the scientific progress of mankind.

Modern Priests

As discussed earlier, the wisest men worked as priests. Until a few decades ago, those wise priests also lived in darkness. They were not even aware of basic science. Priests did not know whether the sun revolved around the earth or vice versa. No one under the sun knew the cause of diseases. Before Pasteur, no priest could imagine that tiny bacteria living on pets, were responsible for deadly diseases.

They did whatever they could to wrestle with diseases. They had no remedy for many of the ailments, so they blamed divine powers for those diseases.

Not only common priests, the most enlightened prophets of the world were also engulfed in darkness. For example, Moses began a quest for figuring out the cause of the plagues. He could not imagine that the tiny bacteria living on rats could be the reason behind the mighty plagues. He meditated and discovered that some superpower in the sky inflicted such mass killing. Moses proclaimed that the plagues were caused by the wrath of that power.

The Buddha, a genius of his time, could not have a vision that tiny organisms living comfortably on the domestic animals were behind human suffering. He meditated for years just to discover the cause of human sufferings. At last, he discovered that all human miseries were punishments for sins committed in the previous birth.

Jesus worked as a faith healer throughout his life. He was known for his healing touch. His divine powers lay in his ability to cure diseases. He too could not dream that leprosy was an attack of billions of small unseen bacteria. Jesus wisely announced that all diseases were caused by demonic possession. Authors of the Bible wrote that Jesus himself cast the demons away using his divine powers, and cured many patients.

Let us consider how Moses, the Buddha and Jesus treated their patients, for example, what they prescribed for a patient suffering from leprosy? Moses believed that diseases were caused by violation of the Ten Commandments. The Bible mentions that Moses prescribed bird and animal sacrifices for the lepers. These sacrifices appeased God, and he cured the lepers.

The Buddha believed that diseases were punishment of the violence men had committed during their previous births. He advised his patients to follow non-violence that would ensure good health in their next birth. This way, the Buddha treated only the diseases of the next birth!

Jesus believed that leprosy was caused by some demon. The Bible mentions that Jesus treated leprosy patients through his magical spells. He cast the demon of leprosy away. Today, these remedies seem amusing. Were Moses, the Buddha and Jesus lying or fooling their patients? Not at all, they all were truthful. In fact, they had no microscope to identify the culprits. They had no X-ray or ultrasound machine to see through the human body.

Let's imagine Moses, the Buddha and Jesus revisiting the earth. How would they cure leprosy today? Would they still prescribe sacrifices and other spiritual cures? How would they react to modern evidence-based medicine? They would study modern medicine first; soon, they would realize their ignorance. After experiencing the efficacy of modern remedies, they would discard their previous teachings. They would diagnose the skin lesion of the patient and treat accordingly.

However, today's priests are different. They teach ancient knowledge to the people, but rely on modern medicine for themselves. Many modern priests prefer five-star hospitals for their treatment. On the contrary, they teach the theory of sins and advise prayers, donations and meditation to the devotees. They take their children for polio vaccination in the morning; but in the evening, they teach a polio patient that his disease was a result of his sins. Priests would themselves have only two children, but advise the people that children are God's gifts.

There are many examples where modern priests are seen enjoying various inventions of science but they do not advise their disciples to be scientific. The priests teaching through TV communicate their lectures through scientific apparatuses. They must have the basic knowledge of science. How can they then say that God gave birth to Adam and Eve six thousand years ago? Why don't they know that science has discarded the theory of special creation? Why don't they acknowledge that human skeletons belonging to two hundred thousand years ago have been excavated?

There are two kinds of darkness. First is the darkness of night with no source of light. Ancient priests were living in such darkness. The second type of darkness can be perceived in broad daylight if one's eyes are closed. Modern priests are living in the second type of darkness and are persuading their pupils to do the same.

Modern priests claim themselves to be learned. On the contrary, they do not understand the meaning of even the religious books. They do not know the history of religion. The priests appearing in public meetings or TV are supposed to be well informed. Before preaching religion, one must read science. During all the periods, religions began where scientific discoveries ended. To teach religion without the knowledge of science is similar to teaching a degree class without going to school at all.

For example, modern priests claim to treat many mental and physical illnesses through meditation. They narrate precisely how the sins of previous births are behind human disease. They are frequently treating patients of cancer through blessings. However, they must have the knowledge of modern science before they make such claims.

After reading the recent advances about cancer, only a fool can think of treating a cancer patient by blessing him. At times, some of these priest are well informed but practise chicanery. Today, modern science has discovered the cause of almost all the diseases prevalent in society. It has discarded the theory of sins, the gods and the demons behind illnesses. Thus, most modern priests advocating the sin theory are intentionally fooling people.

In fact, modern priests work professionally. Today, religions are like giant corporations where many priests work as service providers on behalf of the gods. To learn a profession one needs years of rigorous study. Priesthood – the most respected profession – requires no training or a degree. One has to show faith and devotion towards gods. One has to mug up the couplets from ancient scriptures; regardless of whether one understands their meaning. One must master the art of oration of ancient stories.

The more promises one can make on behalf of gods (good priests do not make any promises themselves), the more successful as a priest he is. An ideal priest must be blind to reason, history and science. A person with common sense, logic, reasoning and love for truth should not try to become a priest. He will spoil the broth cooking in temples.

Businesses run by priests can be visualized through an example. The example of Hinduism is the best to illustrate this. There are millions of employees on the payroll of the Hindu Gods Inc. India has around one thousand big and famous temples. These temples are located in different states of India. Almost every day, millions of people visit these temples often travelling long distances. Thus, they waste lots of money and time.

Most of these temples are 50–100 years old. The priests of these temples have popularized stories about these temples. For example, some god visited the temple during old times or some magic happened in this temple. Many past visitors have received blessings. Furthermore, visiting these temples will fulfil your dreams. Many such myths attract the masses to visit those temples.

These temples are such big sources of income that they feed a large number of people of the towns where these are situated. These temples usually have fifty to one hundred priests. They alone are authorized to take donations on behalf of the deity installed there. These temples remain crowded throughout the year; therefore, their priests charge bribes to allow the devotees to reach the idol.

Their priests welcome and bless rich and popular devotees who can provide them more wealth. On the contrary, they harass and insult the poor. Many priests of the Hindu temples do not consider all devotees as equals. Thus, they violate the core teaching of all religions – equality.

Many priests of these temples behave like the commissioning agents of gods. They manage contractual worship to fulfil specific wishes of the rich. The administrators of such temples, a group of priests, publicly declare the cost of different rituals. In the evening, these priests distribute the common donation to the temple among themselves. They can be commonly seen fighting for their share.

A few of these are caught sexually exploiting female devotees in the process of blessing them with children. Many such priests are seen intoxicated within the temple. Thus, many of the priests exhibit greed, discrimination, adultery and intoxication under the nose of the gods. Had the gods been inside the temples, they would have punished the sinners or at least expelled them from the temple.

Other than priests, hundreds of other employees also work in each of these temples as sweepers, watchmen, etc. Around one thousand people are employed outside these temples as vendors of sweets, flowers and garlands. Many people find employment in the hotels and restaurants nearby.

There you may also find hundreds of vendors of blessings – the beggars. Each temple thus becomes a source of livelihood for a few thousand families. Besides, India also has many thousands of medium-sized temples. Each such temple feeds a few hundred families. Thus a substantial percentage of the Hindu population earns its livelihood from the Hindu Gods Inc. The large number of devoted employees of the temples is the most important reason behind the flourishing business of the Hindu Gods Inc.

For example, suppose, some Hindu god himself approaches the priests to close the temples and advises the people to worship in their homes. The priests would never accept this proposal. They would protest: who would donate money to them? Who would purchase sweets, garlands, etc? Who would give donations to the beggars? The priests would not recognize such a god.

Soon, the priests would declare that god a cheat. They would show the real god standing in the centre of the temple – the idol. The priests would argue that the idol is the real god since people donated money to him. The idol has been nourishing them for many generations; they cannot accept any Tom, Dick or Harry as their god.

Besides, the business of priests is dependent upon helplessness, fear, disease, ambition and revenge of the masses. Suffering masses are the real customers of priests. Priests would never like the earth to be transformed into a heaven. Then nobody would come to them to find a remedy for his suffering. Nobody would ask them the way to heaven.

Priests psychologically treat many problems of the masses such as fear, disease, poverty, ambition, etc. For this, priests propagate that patients must have faith in the gods. This faith in the gods is mandatory for the smooth running of the business of priests. Therefore, each priest tries his level best to establish the image of gods as almighty and caring. For this, they frequently fabricate stories about gods. Today, almost all people are concerned about their business, so are priests – the only beneficiaries of the concept of gods.

Besides the priests in temples, an exclusively new class of modern Hindu priests has flourished with the expansion of the TV network. Common priests of today hardly understand the original script of the Rig Veda, the Ramayana or the Puranas. Today, a handful of modern priests explain the ancient books in some public meeting or through many religious channels. These modern priests, the five-star priests or Babas as they are commonly known are worshipped as gods. They are as famous as cricketers and film stars. Today, most devotees receive religious knowledge through these five-star priests.

All these Babas are excellent orators. Firstly, they all propagate that the stories mentioned in ancient religious books are history. At the same time, they never tell the time period of the stories. The story, whose time of happening is not known, cannot be history. For example, many such Babas narrates the story of Ram frequently. None of them ever tell year of birth of Ram.

While narrating the old texts, they weave words and garnish them. They exaggerate in order to explain and prove that the unbelievable stories of ancient books had actually happened. They present such a live depiction of the old stories as if they were eyewitnesses. They do not hesitate to lie in the process.

The process can be understood through one example. One such Baba regularly teaches 'Shiva' meditation on TV. The slogan of his organization reads: 'The Baba teaches the Vedic techniques of meditation that neutralize the sins of the previous births.' During the oration of the Baba, this slogan appears as a caption on the TV screen almost every minute. This is done to convince the devotees that the Baba is teaching the Vedic techniques of meditation.

The Vedas describe Lord Shiva as a name of the sky god Indra or Rudra. The meditation he teaches is nowhere mentioned in any Veda. Besides, the Vedas do not mention the theory of punishment for sins of previous births. The Vedas do not advise any such meditation to neutralize the sins of previous births. It was the Buddha who taught that the sins of the previous birth are punished in this life. The Buddha came centuries after the Vedas were written. However, none of the learned Vedic scholars seem to point out this discrepancy.

The Baba proclaims that through his meditation, the devotees can escape punishment for their sins. The Hindu god normally punishes the sinners after seven births. The Baba is teaching his followers to escape the punishment of the sins they have committed during the seven previous births. Through this, the Baba intends to disturb the divine system that seeks to punish sinners! He is teaching legally imprisoned people to escape from jail. If the credentials of the Baba are so dubious, imagine the rest of his teachings.

For example, he claims that his meditation therapy can heal all human diseases. Apparently, after the therapy his devotees emit positive energies. These energies can kill bacteria in water. These can wash each cell of the human body. Apart from curing illnesses, these energies can help to pass examinations, avoid traffic jams, solve marital problems and all the human dilemmas under the sun. These energies can be perceived by human eyes and cameras. The Baba narrates the example of a group of his devotees who meditated in a dark hall. Before meditation, the devotees emitted blue light but after the meditation they emitted yellow light.

For the purpose of meditation, he teaches hymns composed by himself. One of the hymns reads: 'I accept myself; I forgive myself; I love myself unconditionally.' To treat the illness, the patient has to recite such hymn many times, while concentrating on the diseased organ. This process will apparently heal the patient. After the Baba teaches this, another caption appears on the screen. It reads: 'He is the father of the art of healing.' The designation of the father of some concept is normally reserved for the pioneer of that concept. Thus some ancient priest deserves this distinguished title.

Many times, these Babas use analogies to explain religious concepts. For example, one Baba says that gods keep the record of your good and bad deeds, just as telephone companies keep the record of telephone calls. Your credit balance increases through good deeds, and bad deeds are like the calls made.

These Babas proclaim that their lives are devoted to the service of humanity. On the contrary, they charge the organizers handsomely. Usually, the cost of their one-hour oration is around a million rupees. The organizers prefer the teachers with a larger following, since lectures of the popular ones attract more people and thus more money through donations. Do you think that Moses, the Buddha or Jesus charged money for their teachings? Since they lectured for free, they were not concerned about the number of persons who listened to them. On the other hand, modern teachers are concerned with the numbers of their followers.

To attract followers, these Babas behave like skilled politicians during their orations. For example, they know that most of their devotees are aged people. They never forget to appreciate the elderly. Priests always advise one to respect one's parents and elders. This is already known to most people who have been taught this since childhood.

They propagate that people can propitiate the gods through the service of their parents. Parents try their best to convey this message to their sons and daughters-in-law. Since the crowd usually has a large concentration of middle-aged ladies, the Babas also crack some Sas Bahu (mother-in-law vs daughter-in-law) jokes and dole out advice about such relationships.

These Babas are aired on TV and use make-up to look divine. They sit on thrones prepared by their devotees. The background displays portraits of gods. In fact, these Babas properly plan their appearance on TV. This simulates the imagined appearance of gods sitting in heaven. To make their orations interesting, they crack jokes at regular intervals.

One of them has developed a successful comic style, as brilliant as any professional comedian. He begins his oration with some serious problem and takes a break after a spell of ten to fifteen minutes. He ends such a spell of oration with a consistent slogan: 'Ab to Jai Ramji ki bolna padega' (Now, you have to recite: Victory be to Ram). He and his followers laugh after each slogan, awakening the drowsy listeners. God Ram is already a victor; there is no need to wish him!

Although these Babas oppose scientific inventions they enjoy the fruits of science regularly. They use most modern methods of communication and transport. They do not look towards the sky for treatment of their illnesses. They do not rely on meditation for their illnesses. They enjoy the best kind of medical services for their ailments and use cosmetic enhancements of their personality.

They live in well-equipped palatial houses. Their lifestyle matches the lifestyle of business tycoons. Many such Babas earn in millions. Nevertheless, they beseech the masses to live a life of contentment and sacrifice. In fact, these Babas are not even truthful to their own gods and religion. They are like clever sales agents. These Babas do their publicity through various TV channels; therefore, they pay a hefty amount to these channels for telecasting their orations. Not only Hindus, the priests of other religions are also running similar businesses on behalf of gods.

Many well-read priests of today do not believe in gods. They are aware of the truth, but they never deny the existence of god. Why would they lie and cheat if they feared reprimand from their gods?

These Baba's are acutely aware of the masses' dependency on the gods. Therefore they never make a concerted effort to be truthful. Such priests will continue to exist as long as they are seen as the spokespersons of gods. The people have to make sincere efforts to find out the truth, and enlighten themselves. For this, they simply have to read the ancient books of their religion themselves.

Today, every country has a censor board as a watchdog to prevent nudity, violence, etc. on TV. News channels are responsible enough to ensure the authenticity of news before being telecast. On the contrary, there is no rational organization to monitor the religious teachers. There must be a censor board presiding over the lectures of these modern priests.

Expectation of Magic in Human Mind

During ancient times, men created and worshipped many gods out of fear and the desire to curry their favour. Today, men face different challenges and fears. Ancient people expected food, shelter and rain from gods. Modern people look towards the gods for their career, ambition, love and revenge. These men are not satisfied with the results in proportion to their efforts; but they still wait for miracles. Modern men expect miracles from gods to fulfil their never-ending desires. They believe that they themselves cannot fulfil their desires.

In fact, many modern men are waiting for some miracles to happen. Therefore, whenever they hear about some miracle happening somewhere, they simply rush towards that place. Besides, people believe these rumours because they have already heard about the miracles of gods in ancient times.

To understand this tendency, let us consider an example. On the night of 21 September 1995, a man in New Delhi woke up at 3 a.m. after a strange dream. He dreamt that his beloved god Ganesha was thirsty. He rushed to the nearby temple and, after a heated discussion with the priest, he managed to reach the idol of Ganesha. He offered a spoonful of milk to the idol. Both the devotee and the priest were surprised when the idol began to drink the offered milk.

They both came out of the temple and declared the news. The news spread like wildfire throughout India. Millions of devotees thronged the temples to quench the thirst of their beloved Ganesha. Economic activity came to a standstill that day, and most offices, banks and markets were deserted.

Normally, devotees pour the milk on the idol with a pot. That day, they did not pour milk over the idol. They instead, held a tablespoon of milk to the mouth of Ganesha. This allowed them to observe whether the idol was actually drinking milk or not. Most of them observed that gradually the level of milk in their spoon reduced.

In fact, people tilted their spoons till the milk finished. If someone questioned this trick, he was jostled by the rest of the devotees. After some time, the crowd of devotees reduced, and many scientific people began reaching the temples. Soon, the idols stopped drinking milk.

The chaos resulted in many minor accidents and group clashes. Fortunately, the electronic media and mobile phones were not as developed then. People were informed of the miracle verbally and telephonically. Even if Lord Ganesha was thirsty, why did the people make such haste? One priest was enough for one idol.

The truth is that all the people wanted their wishes to be fulfilled. The devotees were pouring milk to get their wishes fulfilled, not to quench the thirst of Ganesha. If this were to happen today, the modern media would fix cameras inside the temples and discover the illusion. The media is capable of weeding out these illusions, and has managed to control this kind of chicanery.

Till date, no political party, not even secular parties, have demanded an investigation into the causes of the illusion. What happened at that time that the idols began soaking up milk? There are many reasons to believe that it was a chicanery.

The planners must have deputed one staunch believer for each famous temple in each city. Thus, thousands of devotees must have been appointed for the whole country. Each such devotee had to perform a similar task in the temple allotted to him. He had to reach the temple early in the morning and pour simple soap water over the idol to lower its surface tension.

After pouring the soap water, he had to take a spoonful of milk, and touch the idol with the spoon. Since the idol now had low surface tension, milk in the spoon trickled along the surface of the idol. This gave the impression that the idol was drinking milk. Soon, the devotee showed the miracle to the priest of the temple. After this, they both began shouting that Ganesha was drinking milk. This task must have been done by all the appointed devotees simultaneously.

Whosoever saw the scene summoned the people he knew. People came and offered milk to the idol in a spoon. Regular milk offerings maintained the wet surface of the idols. This deception continued as long as the idols remained wet. Thus time and money were wasted, in what was another effort by the priests to establish their gods.

Limitations of Science

Modern science has come a long way from the days of Hippocrates. However, there is still a lot of ground to cover. Despite our ability to diagnose most diseases, we have not found their cures. For example, cancers, AIDS and many such diseases are still the dark fields of modern medicine.

Medical science has increased human lifespan significantly. However, they have not been able to prevent death. This is why the God delusion persists. As long as remedies are not invented for all human sufferings, people will continue to believe in gods. Advancement of science in the future will further open the eyes of the masses, and make them realize the truth behind gods and religions.

Conclusion

The previous chapters have narrated a brief history of religions. After reading them, it becomes obvious that mankind created all the divine powers called gods. These divine powers were the projections of the different fears and needs of men. Men persistently invented new superhuman powers to wrestle with the new challenges they faced. Men began worshipping those powers to please them.

History of religions teaches that a god useful to the people of one period gradually became useless in the next period. Since necessity is the mother of invention, the new human needs necessitated the invention of new powerful gods to work for them. Mankind often replaced an age-old god with a more promising one.

For example, Mesopotamians worshipped the sun and the sky gods around 3000 BCE. Later, they established that the mother goddess and the phallus were responsible for the fertility of their land. They began worshipping these new gods to increase the yield of their crops.

During the first millennium BCE, people suffered from epidemics such as plague. Contemporary priests invented a new god that was causing plague – Yahweh. Consequently, people began worship of

Yahweh, and forgot the mother goddess, the phallus and the nature gods. Around the second century CE, the masses required a god that could magically cure their miseries. Soon, the kind God of Jesus replaced the cruel Yahweh.

In another example, around 5,000 years ago and also thereafter, the ancient Indians worshipped the sun, the sky, and fire. Around 2,500 years ago, the moral teachings of the Buddha impressed the masses more than the age-old nature gods. After the Buddha, the Indian masses preferred their gods in human shape. Gradually, the sun and the sky god were portrayed in human shapes as Vishnu and Shiva respectively.

Later, Vishnu himself was replaced by his more promising human incarnations such as Ram and Krishna. During the last fifty years, the fashion of changing one's god became very popular. Hindus designated several modern priests as gods. Today, anyone surrounded by followers is considered a god. Today, these modern gods are doing fine business, whose prosperity is directly proportional to their false promises.

Thus, historians and anthropologists have attested that human creative imagination gave rise to religions, similar to writing fiction. In fact, ancient priests wrote fictitious religious literature to teach moral lessons but the subsequent generations took them to be history.

Modern men have adopted the word of science in almost all fields of activity. However, they still follow ancient religious concepts. In their view antiquity reflects the authenticity of the work. The older the temple, the holier it is; the older the religious book, the more authentic it is.

Many modern devotees believe that during ancient times their gods routinely visited the earth and exhibited their magical powers. Many are convinced that the gods and priests of the ancient times were more knowledgeable and technologically advanced.

For example, Hindus believe that ancient Vedas contain some scientific facts which are yet to be discovered. Around 5,000 years ago, the Hindu god Ram maintained his personal aircraft called the Pushpak Viman. Many such prejudices do not let the people reach the truth.

What was fiction in the past has become history today. History of religions can differentiate between fiction and actual events. Thus, history of religions can reveal the truth behind the creation of gods.

The human race was in its infancy during ancient times. Humans lived under constant fear, both seen and unseen. Men had to wrestle with hunger, adverse weather and wild animals, just for survival. Early men were as violent as wild animals. The fear of god compelled them to live peacefully with each other.

Prophets such as Moses, the Buddha and Jesus gradually transformed the wild man into a social animal. Mankind is indebted to these masters for building a peaceful society. Mankind fought many wars for religions, but religions established harmony at least among their devotees.

Moses preached the Ten Commandments to found a civilized society. The Buddha advocated non-violence and thus established a social order. Jesus said: 'Do unto others as thou would have them do unto thee.' It is the core of all the relationships till today. Valmiki guided the masses to behave through the example of the ideal character of Ram. Muhammad authenticated all the previous prophets, and thus gave a message that they all worshiped one God. Besides this, many similar saints taught the lesson of non-violence all over the globe. They guided the masses to behave.

Thus, by and large, the prophets attempted to create a society of peace, equality and justice. Non-violence was the central theme of all religions. Even after many daring voices against violence, many people could not change themselves. The human race is considered civilized today, but many people have not been able to tame the wild animal in themselves. Despite the efforts of the prophets, many people remained violent. They found out ways to fight, through the loopholes in their religion. Renowned author Karen Armstrong has said: 'Like any other human activity, religion can be abused, but it seems to have been something that we have always done.'

History is witness to many non-violent prophets whose devotees committed major atrocities. For example, Jesus abhorred even animal sacrifices, but his followers converted, killed and enslaved many people in the world. The Buddha advised strict non-violence, but his followers killed many animals to eat. The Buddha forbade anyone to worship him. Today, his idols are worshipped throughout the world.

Long ago, human conflicts revolved around the basic needs such as food, sex and shelter. That struggle for survival was sane and rational. For the last 2,000 years, people all over the globe fought for tenuous reasons. They fought to prove that their religion and gods were more powerful and genuine. People of one state made syndicate under the banner of their religion; they attacked other states. They forced the people of other religions to follow their religion and worship their gods. What were the motives behind such barbaric activities? Why did the devotees of Jesus violate his core teachings? Why did the devotees of Moses refuse to follow the Ten Commandments?

In fact, subsequent priest changed their doctrines to curry favour with kings. The priests initiated new practices. They propagated that every devotee must try to spread his religion as this pious activity would lead them to heaven. History has witnessed many people who have devoted their entire lives to spread their religion.

These devotees spread their religions through fear and greed. To prove their gods superior, they even violate the concept of non-violence – the core of their own religion. Medieval history has countless examples of conversion of the vanquished. During that period, either pious kings or priests ruled; they both used religion to fulfil their ambitions. They gathered men for their armies by claiming divine cause. Gradually, forced conversions became popular. Appropriating followers became the sole motive of most religions. The priests and kings fought countless wars for their religion. Their gods had nothing to do with these wars. All the wars were the result of human ambition. Why did the priests and the kings fight wars for religion? Their soldiers were taught that they were fighting a holy war for protection of their religion. They also believed that their death in such a war would allow them to enter heaven.

After each war, the winners forcefully converted the defeated. They were forced to worship the god of the winners. Usually, young women were sent to the harem and males were enslaved.

All tribal religions had many gods; so the followers were always ready to accept new gods. All over the globe, tribal religions were gradually replaced by monotheism – belief in existence of one God. Monotheists were developed and organized and, therefore, they could enslave the tribes. The books of monotheistic religions asserted that there is only one God and there is no other gods.

Since there was no other god, the devotees of the monotheistic religions set out on a quest for teaching about God to the infidels. This doctrine led to many religious wars, and the death of many innocent men.

There are three monotheistic religions in the world: Judaism, Christianity and Islam. Devotees of all three believed that there was only one God in the world. Jews believed that Yahweh was the only god. Christians proclaimed another God – the father of Jesus. Muslims insisted that Allah was the only god. All these claims together, however, points to the existence of three gods.

Jews propagated that Yahweh was the only god and the other two (God and Allah) did not exist. Christians and Muslims made similar declarations. They fought many battles to solve this dispute.

This is absurd because it seems rather obvious that God, Allah and Yahweh are the same name for an ultimate divine power. The holy Koran states that Allah is the same god worshipped by Abraham, Moses and Jesus. It also shares a few fables with the Bible.

The trend of fanaticism and religious warfare cannot only be confined to the pages of history. Terrorism in the late twentieth and early twenty-first century is an outgrowth of fundamentalism and religious intolerance.

The motives of terrorists are rather obscure. Why would people (often educated and prosperous) endanger their lives? What are they going to achieve by killing the innocent?

Do the blessings offered by religion even compare with the value of life? Is heaven a reasonable reward for death?

Fundamentalism is a conviction that is developed by teaching. Fundamentalists start to imbue these values from childhood, so much so that they become a part of the individual's character. Some of them preach that violence in the name of God is holy, and martyrdom in his name will open the doors to heaven.

Children, who show the religious ambitions, are taught many stories of religious wars. Soldiers who died for the cause of religion are glorified. Priests narrate how these martyrs are living in heaven happily. These children are motivated daily with the idea that they also have to safeguard their religion and thus their god. They are taught that they need not fear death; their pious deed will ensure them a place in heaven. Thus, many children develop a burning desire to dedicate their life to religion.

These are the children who may turn out to be suicide bombers. After they grow up, some of them may tie bombs round their waists with a conviction that they would find themselves in heaven immediately after the explosion. Heaven and only heaven can attract someone to suicide.

Normally, a devotee could achieve heaven after practising stern moral behaviour for his whole life. On the other hand, any young suicide bomber can achieve heaven decades earlier than his peers, only after committing a minute's act of criminal bravery. Thus, to achieve heaven, it is wiser to work for one moment instead of following rigorous morals for decades. Therefore, many terrorists are willing to dedicate their life to religion.

Just a few decades ago, fundamentalism was gradually reducing. All over the globe, the light of science was guiding people to come out of the age-old superstitions. However, during the last two decades, activities of religious terrorists increased and they committed many massacres. After these killings of innocents, the intelligentsia of the earth is less sanguine about the success of truth over superstitions. Are terrorists going to rule the planet earth again! Contrary to the past, today's fundamentalists are equipped with modern weapons and therefore have the potential of destroying the earth. Mankind has to eradicate fundamentalism to continue in their heavenly abode.

Today, fundamentalism and its product terrorism are big threats to the security of the globe. Mankind has to eradicate these diseases, since these have the potential to destroy the earth.

Fundamentalism is an outcome of illiteracy, poverty and conditioning from childhood. We must endeavour to spread secular education.

Religion is not intrinsic to man. No child is born with the knowledge of religion. But society shapes its new generations according to the knowledge and belief system it follows. Each child acquires the knowledge of its own religion through teachings of its parents, priests and peers. To devise a hatred-free society, future generations must be enriched with authentic knowledge about the history of gods. School books must teach the origin of life, anthropology and a brief history of each religion. This knowledge may vaccinate the readers against the disease of religious terrorism.

Today, these topics are dealt with in books of sixth to twelfth standard in several countries. Normally, the content of these books are not enough. The books must elaborate on these topics at length. Furthermore, parents and teachers often obstruct the analysis of the fallacies in religion. Knowledge of these issues will ensure that future generations are better informed and less susceptible to religion.

As discussed earlier also, religions posed a hurdle to the growth of science. However, the Renaissance challenged the norm and paved the way for an era of enterprise and free thought.

In the last one hundred years, science has managed to create a heaven on earth. Science has made it possible to feed more than six billion people. A century ago, the same food was available to only rare fortunate people. Today, in most countries, obesity is common, and starvation is rare. Common man can afford luxuries that even kings could not dream of a hundred years ago.

Furthermore, science has almost eradicated many social diseases such as slavery, women exploitation and child labour. It has also devised many new ways to effectively control many crimes and ensure justice; thereby, reducing the fear of masses. Enforcement of democracy also finds its roots in scientific methods. Science has given a different kind of freedom to mankind.

Development of media has played a major role in enforcement of law, justice, democracy and human rights. Media could develop only with the help of modern information technology. The media today can communicate any interesting news to almost the whole world within minutes of its happening. You can now talk and see a person standing on the opposite side of the globe. You can now visit space on vacation. In fact, scientific advancements of today defy description.

To maintain this luxurious lifestyle, mankind needs sources of energy such as petrol, coal or electricity. These were produced by the energy of the sun over a long period of time. In the last 100 years, mankind consumed almost half the fossil fuels that the sun produced in two billion years.

To live in this heavenly abode, men have to learn to utilize solar energy and atomic energy more efficiently. The human race has to cultivate such a behaviour which hurts neither any living being nor the environment.

Have you ever thought why there are many religions and there is only one science on the earth? Devotees of different religions follow different customs, rituals, prayers, attributes of gods, etc. Each religion has many sects; these sects are further divided as per the geographical locations of the devotees. Thus, religious concepts of different people are altogether different. For example, people of one religion sacrifice animals to appease their gods; whereas, people of other religion appease their gods through the service of those animals. To take another example, the idol worship is core of one religion; whereas, the other religion has imposed a taboo over idol worship. One can say that this discrepancy among religions is due to the fact that religions originated in different geographical locations.

Not only religion, science was also conceived by the scientists of diverse origin. However, all those unconnected scientists discovered exactly similar scientific principles. Have you ever heard Indian science, British science or American science? All over the world, many pioneer scientists discovered their principles and later other scientists attested those. If some principle was found incorrect, soon its inventor accepted the truth.

There is one concrete reason behind the existence of many religious concepts and only one science on the earth. About one thing or concept, there is only one truth but there can be many lies.

Today, mankind has to conceive a global religion of humanity. All the countries have to write a new Bible of international rules and regulations.

Man conceived and worshipped all the gods as his creator and nurturer. Scientists have discovered that sunrays that fell on the oceanic water gave rise to life, and kept the earth warm enough to survive. The energy of the sun makes all the food, oxygen, drinking water and fuel that we consume today. It thus seems far better to revere the sun, the scientifically proven creator and nurturer of life.

Select Bibliography

1. Life after Death

1. Armstrong, Karen, *A History of God*, New York: Ballantine Books, 1994.
2. Darlington, C.D., *The Evolution of Man and Society*, London: George Allen & Unwin Ltd, 1971.
3. Ember, Carol R., Melvin Ember, and Peter N. Peregrine, *Anthropology*, Delhi: Pearson Education, 2003.
4. Kavanaugh, James, *The Birth of God*, New York: Trident Press, 1969.
5. Mellars, Paul, and Chris Stringer, *The Human Revolution*, Edinburgh: Edinburgh University Press, 1989.
6. Mithen, Steven, *The Prehistory of Mind*, London: Thames & Hudson, 1996.
7. Tylor, Edward B., 'Animism' (Originally published in 1871), in William A. Lessa and Evon Z. Vogt (eds), *Reader in Comparative Religion: An Anthropological Approach*, 4th ed., New York: Harper & Row, 1979.
8. Watson, Peter, *IDEAS (A History from Fire to Freud)*, London: Weidenfeld & Nicolson, 2005.
9. Winston, Robert, *The Story of God*, London: Bantam Press, 2005.

2. Birth of Gods

1. Armstrong, Karen, *A History of God*, New York: Ballantine Books, 1994.

2. Basham, A.L., *The Wonder That Was India*, New Delhi: Picador, 2004.

3. Darlington, C.D., *The Evolution of Man and Society*, London: George Allen & Unwin Ltd, 1971.

4. Ember, Carol R., Melvin Ember, and Peter N. Peregrine, *Anthropology*, Delhi: Pearson Education, 2003.

5. Fagan, Brian, *The Great Journey*, London & New York: Thames & Hudson, 1987.

6. Hammond, Mason, *The City in the Ancient World*, Cambridge, Massachusetts: Harvard University Press, 1972.

7. Mithen, Steven, *The Prehistory of Mind*, London: Thames & Hudson, 1996.

8. Parrinder, Geoffrey, *World Religions*, New York: Facts on File Publication, 197 1.

9. Redford, D., *Akhenaten, The Heretic King*, Princeton: Princeton University Press, 1994.

10 Watson, Peter, *IDEAS (A History from Fire to Freud)*, London: Weidenfeld & Nicolson, 2005.

11. Winston, Robert, *The Story of God*, London: Bantam Press, 2005.

3. Learning to Survive

1. Cauvin, Jacques, *The Birth of the Gods and the Origin of Agriculture*, Cambridge, England: Cambridge University Press, 2000.

2. Cohen, Mark Nathan, *The Food Crisis in Prehistory*, New Haven: Yale University Press, 1977.

3. Darlington, C.D, *The Evolution of Man and Society*, London: George Allen and Unwin Ltd, 1971.

4. Ember, Carol R., Melvin Ember and Peter N. Peregrine, *Anthropology*, New Delhi: Pearson Education, 2003.

5. Gimbutas, Marija, *The Gods and Goddesses of Old Europe: 6500-3500 BC*, London: Thames & Hudson, 1982.

6. Harris, David R., (ed.), *The Origin and Spread of Agriculture and Pastoralism in Eurasia*, London: University College of London Press, 1996.

7. Jevons, Frank B., *An Introduction to the History of Religions*, London: Methuen, 1896/1904.

8. Vangaard, Thorkil, *Phallos: A Symbol and its History in the Male World*, London: Jonathan Cape, 1969.

9. Watson, Peter, *IDEAS (A History from Fire to Freud)*, London: Weidenfeld & Nicolson, 2005.

4. Learning to Write

1. Basham, A. L., *The Wonder That Was India*, New Delhi: Picador, 2004.

2. *Encyclopaedia Britannica*, 2007 Ultimate Reference Suite, Chicago: 2007.

3. Jevons, Frank B., *An Introduction to the History of Religions*, London: Methuen, 1896/1904.

4. Parrinder, Geoffrey, *World Religions*, New York: Facts on File Publication, 197 1.

5. Redford, D., *Akhenaten, The Heretic King*, Princeton: Princeton University Press, 1994.

6. Watson, Peter, *IDEAS (A History from Fire to Freud)*, London: Weidenfeld & Nicolson, 2005.

5. Sacrifice: Bribing the Gods

1. Dalal, Roshen, *The Penguin Dictionary of Religions in India*, New Delhi: Penguin Books, 2006.

2. *Encyclopaedia Britannica*, 2007 Ultimate Reference Suite, Chicago: 2007.

3. James, King, *The Holy Bible, Old Testament, Genesis*, New York: The Random House Publishing Group, 1991.

4. Kerkes, Royden Keith, *Sacrifice in Greek and Roman Religions and Early Judaism*, London: Adam and Charles Black, 1953.

5. Parrinder, Geoffrey, *World Religions*, New York: Facts on File Publication, 1971.

6. Watson, Peter, *IDEAS (A History from Fire to Freud)*, London: Weidenfeld & Nicolson, 2005.

7. Winston, Robert, *The Story of God*, London: Bantam Press, 2005.

6. Gods and Demons of Diseases

1. Ember, Carol R., Melvin Ember and Peter N. Peregrine, *Anthropology*, Delhi: Pearson Education, 2003.

2. Finley, M.I. (tr.), *The Viking Portable Greek Historians*

3. Hammond, Mason, *The City in the Ancient World*, Cambridge, Massachusetts: Harvard University Press, 1972.

4. James, King, *The Holy Bible, Old Testament, Leviticus*, New York: The Random House Publishing Group, 1991.

5. Millidge, Judith, *The Handbook of Dreams*, China: Silverdale Books, 2003.

6. Stubbs, S.G.B, *Magic to Medicine*, London: Thrift Books, 1951.

7. Watson, Peter, *IDEAS (A History from Fire to Freud)*, London: Weidenfeld & Nicolson, 2005.

7. Hinduism

1. Basham, A. L., *The Wonder That Was India*, New Delhi: Picador, 2004.

2. Dalal, Roshen, *The Penguin Dictionary of Religion in India*, New Delhi: Penguin Books, 2006.

3. Lal, Makkhan, *Ancient India*, New Delhi: NCERT Books, 2002.

4. Ralph, T. H. Griffith (tr.), *The Hymns of the Rigveda*, Delhi: Motilal Banarsidass Publishers, 2004.

5. Samradh, Anand, *The Buddha, The Essence of Dhamma and Its Practice*, New Delhi: 2005.

6. Thapar, Romila, *The Penguin History of Early India*, New Delhi: Penguin Books, 2003.

7. Uppal, Shweta (ed.), *Our Past*, Part I, New Delhi: NCERT Books, 2005.

8. Watson, Peter, *IDEAS (A History from Fire to Freud)*, London: Weidenfeld & Nicolson, 2005.

8. Judaism

1. Armstrong, Karen, *A History of God*, New York: Ballantine Books, 1994.

2. James, King, *The Holy Bible, Old Testament, Genesis*, New York: The Random House Publishing Group, 1991.

3. Parrinder, Geoffrey, *World Religions*, New York: Facts on File Publication, 197 1.

4. Winston, Robert, *The Story of God*, London: Bantam Press, 2005.

9. Christianity

1. Armstrong, Karen, *A History of God*, New York: Ballantine Books, 1994.

2. James, King, *The Holy Bible, New Testament*, New York: The Random House Publishing Group, 1991.

3. Stubbs, S.G.B., *Magic to Medicine*, London: Thrift Books, 1951.

10. Origin of Life

1. Darlington, C.D., *The Evolution of Man and Society*, London: George Allen and Unwin Ltd, 1971.

2. Ember, Carol R., Melvin Ember and Peter N. Peregrine, *Anthropology*, Delhi: Pearson Education, 2003.

3. Hickman, B. P., L. S. Roberts, and F. M. Hickman, *Integrated Principles of Zoology*, New York: Times Mirror/ Mosby College Publishing, 1984.

4. Parrinder, Geoffrey, *World Religions*, New York: Facts on File Publication, 1971.

Acknowledgements

I express my deep sense of gratitude to Mr S.K. Ray Chaudhuri for editing the book meticulously. I am short of words to describe the marathon efforts of Shantanu Ray Chaudhuri at HarperCollins; without him I could not have reached this stage. I am grateful to Prof. Surinder Nath for his encouragement. I would like to thank Mr Radha Krishna and Ms Neha Madan for their editorial advice.

I wish to thank my colleagues Dr Dharmendra Kumar Kansal and Dr Vijay Kumar Sharma for their cooperation and faith. The manager of my clinic, Ms Ritu Gupta, deserves special admiration. She took up a lot of my professional responsibilities, that too with great care precision, for the last five years. Sunder, my chauffeur and caretaker, who facilitated my working even on wheels, deserves words of appreciation. I am thankful to other staff members such as Parmanand, Vinod, Manish and Ashok for their active cooperation.

Last but not the least, I thank my mother and daughter, who encouraged my writing despite their deep faith in God.

Dr Ajay Kansal
Professor of Pathology
Saraswati Institute of Medical Sciences
Hapur, UP, India